Where Is Everybody?

ALSO BY MYRTIE BARKER

I am only one
Parade of days

Where

Is

Everybody?

Myrtie Barker

THE BOBBS-MERRILL COMPANY, INC.
A Subsidiary of Howard W. Sams & Co., Inc., Publishers
INDIANAPOLIS • KANSAS CITY • NEW YORK

Acknowledgments

Listing all the people who have nurtured this book into being is well-nigh impossible. Special gratitude, however, is due my niece Cynthia Barker Johnson and my friend Genevieve Weaver, both of whom helped with the typing.

Further appreciation is extended also to those who have lent encouragement from time to time . . . my cousin Billie Lawrence; Mrs. Susan M. Ostrom, retired columnist of the Indianapolis *News;* Vivian Beaumont Hoff; Ruth Anderson, artist.

Finally and more especially, The Indianapolis *News,* which was so kind as to release certain previously published material that had appeared in My Window column.

Man dwells apart, though not alone,

    He walks among his peers unread;

The best of thoughts which he hath known

    For lack of listeners are not said.

JEAN INGELOW

Foreword

Adjusting to circumstances is no new thing to any of us. The man, woman, or child does not live who has not found some fly in the ointment.

The constant challenge is in coming to terms with that which would cast a cloud across our sun.

All too often, time and events utterly annihilate a pattern of living, and a lone survivor of a former way of life is left to pick up the fragments. Yes, pick up the fragments and find some degree of happiness in that which is left.

It is either that, or spend the rest of one's days sitting in the ashes.

To all who, perchance, still cannot realize that nothing is permanent except new demands, these lines are directed. If they supply even one answer to one solitary soul, the effort has not been without reward.

MYRTIE BARKER

Contents

1.

Roof To Spare

Few situations present a more desolate appearance than one lone woman living by herself in a big, rambling house—set down in a wide reach of walks and driveways, towering pines, and grass that most of the time needs cutting.

It is sort of ghostly—with the occupant herself playing the part of the ghost.

Of course, the fact that it looks that way does not always mean that it is that way. In truth, that singular specimen of femininity dwelling within may be lavishly enjoying her solitary existence. For the first time in her life, she may be free to let all three dogs sleep on the end of her bed; burn as many lights for as long as she likes; soak in the bathtub for two hours; and have fish for breakfast.

There are certain compensations in eccentricity which any really good hermitess can take unto herself—given the chance. Or that she will gradually and unknowingly develop. It inevitably happens.

You can turn queer very easily when no one is around to suddenly appear and catch you eating your scrambled egg right out of the skillet.

Some people can adequately and intelligently regulate their lives, come what may. They can maintain a sane and cultured decorum whether in a milling mob of humanity or alone two weeks straight in a ten-room house.

There are others, however, who need the discipline of folks about—the nice coziness of somebody bursting in the front door and shouting: "Goll-ee, it's good to be home!"

Of course the moment you decide to take another soul into your domain, you immediately fall victim to certain inhibitions and complications. You may not realize this right away. But by the time the third day's dishes are piled up in the sink, you remember you're not living alone anymore and you had better clean up the place.

Running around until noon in hair rollers and a coffee-besplattered robe is out. And so are untimely inspirations—such as suddenly deciding around two o'clock in the morning to sand the living room floor or run over that real hard cadenza in Rachmaninoff's Third.

With your house, your behavior, your looks, your habits under continual surveillance, you lose the luxury of being either indolent or erratic. And this is reason enough to cause one to hesitate in taking anybody else under the roof. It is also reason enough to make one do just that.

Too much loneliness, as has been hitherto hinted, makes for an eventual departure from normal, natural standards and procedures. And besides that, it's very nice to have someone around with whom to swap "good mornings" and "good nights." And it's fun to share one's culinary talents, if, on an ambitious impulse, one takes a notion to bake a lemon pie.

A sense of direction is the major need of anybody whose usual pattern of life has been torn asunder. When death's cold hands have reached forth and pulled a stalwart pillar from the structure of your existence, you must have something to tie on to.

Too much freedom can hang heavy. The constant nudge of responsibilities and obligations keeps one moving and awake. If there isn't the sweeper to run, the beds to make, clean towels to put up in the bathroom, strawberries to pick and preserve, stockings to rinse out, and a hem to put in a dress, why get up in the morning?

A few sacrifices and restrictions are likewise healthy; in other words, the lone person should saddle herself with a few reasons why she cannot take off at the drop of a hat. It can be anything from a few puny house plants on a window ledge, to a tinner coming to replace a downspout; a pet hamster that has to be fed, to somebody that has a room in your house and is afraid to stay by herself at night.

It adds to your self-esteem to have certain matters that require your personal presence and attention . . . it gives stature to the ego. Also, others probably look upon you with a little higher regard if you are not too available always.

Really, it was quite a change of pace when the family came.

Immediately after my brother Syd and his little wife Louise got the word that our Papa had left us, they came. They came and brought the three children.

There was Cynthia, eleven. And there was Bruce, six. And there was baby Alan, seven months. With them, of course, came dolls, and model cars, and the crib and the play-pen, and bottles and bottles of formula—plus cans of baby food; and enough clothes for everyone: pinafores and gingham dresses for Cynthia, and little shirts and dungarees for Bruce . . . and, of course, towering heaps of diapers for the baby.

Truly, it is the ultimate offering of love for a young family to

3

suddenly gather up the essentials of their daily life and transport all to another house and other circumstances, particularly when there are all the accouterments of a baby to bring along—like the vaporizer and the talcum powder, rattlers and rubber pants.

But the needs of the living do not cease, even though a dear one has stepped into the misty beyond. Stomachs get empty, and someone has to run to the grocery for bacon; something goes wrong with the car, and the garage man must be called. The mail comes. One of the youngsters climbs up to reach a coat off the top hook in the closet and falls.

And people come—friends and kin. They come and they keep coming. And there is no time even to go to your room and slip into a different dress, or to drink a glass of milk without having to stop to take care of something that needs to be done. No time to think. And this is good. However, even in this mental haze of confusion, you wonder what it will be like when it is all over and you are left alone to grope from room to room.

It was frightening to consider. It must not happen. The lively activity that came from having the family around must go on; the talk and the play and the squealing of the children; the comfort in having Louise near; the strength and the security in Syd's being close at hand. The only hope of the future seemed to be in having them stay.

I asked them if they could come—come for all time.

But Louise and Syd reminded me of their own home, a home atop a hill that they loved. And they must go back to their home just as soon as things settled down. There would be a way. But there seemed to be no door in the gray, impenetrable wall that loomed up ahead.

And then one morning the telephone rang. It was Amy Keene, a retired teacher. Really, our acquaintance had been very slight.

4

We had simply met occasionally at Penwomen meetings. Amy asked if she might come out and spend the afternoon. She had lost her own father some years ago. And she remembered the dismal, empty feeling. She felt that she might have something to say that would help.

Since she had no car, she would have to come out on the bus. This was all very well. But there was no bus back. Amy would have to stay all night.

With someone coming, Louise and Syd decided to take a temporary respite from their loving post of duty. Amy would be on hand for company. So they gathered up the youngsters and the things that they would need overnight and left, for the first time since Papa had gone.

I was watching from my window when Amy, a rather smallish woman, her head tucked down into her coat collar to escape the wind, climbed down from the bus and headed toward our front gate. This would be something of a new experience for both of us . . . meeting, just we two, under different circumstances and in a different environment. Exchanging greetings in the midst of an assembly of women isn't exactly like sitting down and facing each other and making conversation for a time . . . in fact, all evening, clear up to bedtime, during breakfast the following day, and half-way through the morning.

Supper was right ready to put on the table when the visitor arrived. It had been rather soothing and pleasant patting out hamburger into cakes, slashing up a head of lettuce for salad, sticking big Idaho potatoes in the oven to bake, making a batch of chocolate brownies to eat with pineapple sherbet. In the placid routine of preparing a meal—the first cooking on my own in several weeks—there came an inner quietude. Apparently it was true: busy hands do caress and comfort a restless mind.

Suddenly, Mildred Thompson's experience came to mind. For months on end she had been torn with grief after her husband died. There seemed to be no lessening of her dark despair. And then one day Mildred took a look around at her kitchen walls. They were faded and drab. She decided they could use a coat of paint, and that she would do the job herself.

It was while she was on the ladder, whisking the brush to and fro, spreading a path of fresh paint, that something let loose inside, a black gloom lifted, and a kind of sunlight fell on her thoughts. The clouds had parted. And from that instant onward, they continued to part.

In the movement of muscle and bone, the brain must leave one track for another. And in the switch comes relief.

It was a momentary contemplation, as Amy sat down on the opposite side of the supper table. She was almost gay, a lively little woman, retired from her job but not from living. Indeed, she had just gotten back from Alaska. She held up a sheaf of papers.

"You know," she began, "I thought you just might like to hear this article about my trip—and the good news. I just heard from an editor today, and he is taking the article and sending me a check for five hundred dollars."

The news burst on the air like the first strains of music from a marching band. In sheer joy I let out a squeal of delight:

"Oh, Amy! That's wonderful—just wonderful! Please read it. Please!"

"After supper, maybe."

"No, now. I can't wait. Supper can."

And just like that the epical event unfurled. It was an unplanned episode, plopped right down on home territory. And for the time it took to read perhaps three thousand words, thought took flight into another realm. Momentarily, at least, the turmoil and unrest over what to do was stilled by what someone else had done.

Perhaps this was one more prescription for peace: to find excitement in the experience of other people, to take leave of our own lives by looking on and listening. There was escape in simply becoming wholly and completely absorbed in what was transpiring among those whom we knew.

Certainly, Amy's trip to Alaska was no small adventure. And our hamburgers didn't taste too bad warmed over.

We talked of our fathers.

Amy's memory of her own dad and his death was still fresh in her mind, though he had died many years before. "I remember," she said, "how I shut the door to his room. To go in seemed to be something that I would never be able to stand again."

Of course we had had to use Papa's room for the family. The cradle had been put up at one end for baby Alan, with Syd and Louise in the big bed; young Bruce was in the little single bed in the spare bedroom, Cynthia with me in my room.

Amy was silent for a time. And then she added: "You have had a very fine antidote for grief. You have had the diverting influence of young life about you. It is earth's perennial renewal of hope."

She paused, as if to weigh this against that. "You're fortunate," she said. "Really fortunate. I'm not going to worry about you anymore."

Only days later, Sandra Sue, the seven-year-old daughter of my friend Kay, came to spend a day and a night. In fact, she was here when Grandpa, a spry eighty-four, arrived for a week's visit. Said Grandpa to Sandra: "Would you like to know a new way to count to one hundred?"

The little girl nodded her blonde head.

"Well now, pay attention," said Grandpa, revealing his past profession of schoolteacher. "Ten, ten, double ten, forty-five, fifteen."

The youngster looked confused.

Said Grandpa: "Don't you get it? Say it after me."

Sandra repeated the figures as Grandpa gave them out—slowly, thoughtfully. All of a sudden the light dawned. The child jumped to her feet and spun around on her heels: "Goody! Goody!" she cried. "I am going home and tell Mommie and Daddy and Norman. Where did you learn that, Grandpa? You're so smart!"

"Why, thank you," said Grandpa. "I like you, too."

And the days passed . . . one by one. Somehow, it was easier to take life in twenty-four-hour portions . . . or rather, in moment-by-moment hand-outs. It is trying to negotiate with the future that leaves the bereaved dazed and desperate.

It was during Grandpa's visit that the letter came, the letter that was, in its own way, to mark a path for coming years. The name in the left-hand corner, as well as the address, meant nothing at all, meaning that I had never known anyone named Beulah Everett, living at 7999 Willow Branch Drive. However, the lady lost no time in getting to the point. She wrote:

> . . . I read about your Papa. And I am so sorry. You see I know people that know people that know you. And that's how I decided you should have somebody like me to live with you. Nobody should live all by themselves. Only right now, I would like to live with a few less.
>
> You see, I'm hired to fill a kind of grandmotherly role in a family of four young'uns. You know, do the mending, baby

sitting, and listening to lessons at night. Only the young'uns are getting more than an old lady of 74 can take.

Honey, I don't want any pay. I got my social security. I just want a home . . . and something tells me that you would like my company. I can be just awfully comical at times. And besides that, I'm real good at drying dishes. . . .

In other words, putting her hands in a dish pan of suds was out. But, of course, there were all those other virtues. I called Grandpa, who by this time was in the kitchen peeling an apple to eat.

"Mind coming here and listening to a proposal?"

"Man or men?" said Grandpa.

"Neither," I said, and plunged into the letter. Before I had gotten to the "Yours truly" part, Grandpa was rubbing his chin.

"Now, that bears thinking about," he said. "That Beulah person could just very well be an answer to your situation." He rubbed his chin some more. "She just very well could."

Grandpa had gone home by the time Beulah had arranged with one of her acquaintances at church to get her sister's daughter's husband to drive her out. Besides the problems of four lively kids, Beulah had no transportation. It seems that 7999 Willow Branch Drive was in one of those luxurious suburbs set down in the midst of hills and dales, seven curves and five turns from the nearest bus.

And after all, it wouldn't do just now to tell those who were currently issuing a paycheck that she, Beulah Everett, was contemplating leaving, especially for a place where there would be no salary.

Really, it hardly made sense. However, when she appeared at the door, this stranger out of the blue looked as if she had

9

ample I.Q. She was scarcely five foot tall, measuring to the tip-most peak of a pointed green velvet hat. She had a way of tossing her head about as she talked, and the light in her bright brown eyes seemed to keep time.

"Why would you want to leave your present position for simply a home?" It was my first question to Beulah as we sat in the living room and talked, while the husband of the sister of the acquaintance at church waited in the car.

"Right now," said Beulah, "it's the smartest thing I can do. When you are seventy-four that's what you need most—a home, a relaxed and quiet sort of home." She took a deep breath, and her curly head turned quickly as she took in one spot in the living room, and then another.

"That your mamma's portrait up there above the mantel?" I nodded.

"And is that your papa's picture over there?" I nodded again.

"You favor them."

"You're kind."

"I'm what?"

Beulah began to fumble with something just inside the neck of her dress. As she continued to twist and turn some invisible object, her face became more and more strained. Finally, she gave up and dropped her hands in her lap.

"You will have to excuse me," she shouted. "You see, my battery has run down. And I can't hear what you say."

At that she sort of fell back into the chair. There was an awful look of anguish and desperation on her face. She was so short of stature that only the toes of her shoes touched the floor as she sat in a chair. She took off the pointed green velvet hat to tinker with a small round disc inserted in her ear. Tight white ringlets of curls covered her entire head.

"I guess this will have to end our talk," she fairly cried out. "But maybe you could think it over and write to me."

I nodded. And with that Beulah scooted forward and got to her feet as quickly as a woman half her age. She smiled. "You will write?" she said loudly.

Once again I nodded. And Beulah hurried to the door and out to the car waiting in the drive.

That night, lying in bed, I tried to decide.

Certainly, leaving the noise and clamor of four young children to come and live with just one lone woman in a big, quiet house was a change too radical to contemplate. Somehow, Beulah should be made to know something of our background, the story of this big, quiet house and the people who had lived in it. She should know.

And so, in restless fits of slumber, I tried to tell her. Sometimes I was writing with crayon on a huge piece of black art paper. Sometimes the tale was being scribbled on a cloud with a shaking finger.

And then again, I was kneeling by Beulah's chair, shouting into her deaf ears, trying to make her understand.

2.

April Tears

It can happen to anyone.

In fact, if you continue to live and reach old age, you will very likely find yourself all alone. Marriage is no assurance.

A couple can marry and have eleven children. And they can grow up and move to the area of the Yukon, die, or turn indifferent and never come around. After years of hustle and bustle, with little ones all over the place, mornings of leaping out of bed before daylight to put hot food in the stomachs of a small army, nights lying awake while a neighborhood combo rehearses in your front room, life can change. Stealthily, time can slip one member of the family after another across the threshold of the old homeplace into other fields, until, one day, you walk through the house in which you have lived so long, and all is quiet. No one is around. And you recall that everlasting race of days past to lay siege to a mountain of ironing so that there would be clean clothes for everyone; you recall those hectic beginnings of almost every school day, when you joined in the search for lost pencils and galoshes and maybe a spelling book. So often, there was someone sobbing or squealing, or yelling: "Hurry up, the school bus is coming!"

In the thick of all this, your husband might sweetly—or hotly, depending on the mood he happened to be in—ask for a pin. The button was gone off the left cuff of his last clean shirt.

And now all is still.

There is no more slamming of doors, no tennis ball skimming across the ceiling of the kitchen and landing in a pot of vegetable soup.

For those with families, large or small, those husbands and wives who have had no children, only each other, as well as the many single people who have made a home with a sister or brother, aunt, cousin, friend, or aging parents—there comes a day.

In the awful silence of an empty house and an empty life, there comes that plaintive cry : "Where is everybody?"

There is a lonesome little patch just out back beyond the house. It's our garden. It's the place where the sweet corn grew, and the tomatoes, the long green cucumbers and the white squash. And it's all raked up, clean and bare—all ready for the new garden which was to be plowed and planted this year.

We never knew. We never dreamed that this spring would not be like all other springs. We supposed that sometime during the blustery days of March we would, as always, bend over the seed catalogues and, together, make out our order.

Year after year, it had been so. Two pounds Golden Cross sweet corn, one packet Cherry Bell radish, one-half pound golden wax beans, onion plants from Texas, etc.

"The peas are up!" A glad shout would ring across the garden.

"No! Not really!" And I, hanging wet tea towels on the back-yard line, would make straight for the garden and the three rows of Blue Bantam. There we would stand—the gardener and his daughter (Papa and I)— marveling over the miracle wrought by sun and rain, brown earth and Blue Bantam peas: tiny, pale green leaves stretching from one end of the garden to the other, and in no more than seven days since the seeds were dropped into the ground.

But it all reached a climax when the sweet corn was ready. Golden and steaming, plenty of butter, and etiquette be hanged—a time for feasting. Meals were simple when the garden was in its prime. A platter of sweet corn, a platter of tomatoes, and a pitcher of iced tea. And chatter.

Ah, indeed, what is so sweet as two companions—eating as they chat, chatting as they eat? And even then talking about gardening. About the effect of the moon on the growing of crops.

"Plant early potatoes," says superstition, "on St. Patrick's Day or Good Friday, just before the full of the moon . . . and vegetables for leaves, such as cabbage and lettuce, in the new moon . . ."

We didn't want to believe them. We didn't want concur in old moon sayings, but sometimes the experiences in the little plot of ground which was my father's garden made us wonder if, maybe, after all, there was some connection between the heavens and the way the turnips grew.

I can see him now, my beloved gardener, kneeling beside a tomato vine. Maybe pruning, maybe saying a prayer.

We are lonely, the two of us, that little patch of earth which was his garden, and the gardener's daughter. So very lonely.

Just now, I sit at my window—and remember.

And I wonder—is the day really gray, or does the outer view reflect my inner feelings? All the world looks drab and somber.

The clouds are low.

In fact, it would not seem at all impossible to reach up and touch them if, maybe, you were standing on the roof of the house.

That's a fascinating thought, the idea of touching a cloud. I think if I were that near, I would stick my head into the cloud and see what it was like. Would it be the rousing exhilaration usually associated with one's head being in the clouds? Or would it be rain? Or simply more stillness, more mugginess, more grayness?

It is a goodly chance that it would be the last, because a gray day appears to be all-encompassing. It reaches up, down, and around. It hangs over our heads and the horizon; it wraps itself about chimneys and tree tops, and pulls the blinds on the sun. Through the course of the years, we have learned that gray days know no season. They happen in the spring as well as in the winter, in the summer as well as the fall. Sometimes suddenly, sometimes after a night of premeditation, a day decides to be gray. No particular reason, unless perhaps it is nature's way of resting.

A gray day is an effortless day.

Nothing much is going on. No rain. No wind. Just gray. That's the principal characteristic of a gray day. It is simply gray. It is inactive, listless, stubborn. The heavy heavens seem determined to remain gray.

And yet, we can never be sure.

If we are planning a picnic, we go out and look at the sky. We try to guess whether the clouds will part and the sun come through; or whether they will let loose a downpour; or whether things will remain in the status quo—another gray day. But the gray day keeps its secret.

If, however, the picnic is put off, we can take on other chores ideally suited for the days when the sun is on vacation.

Transplanting is best done when it is cloudy. Just now, when the annual seedlings are ready for their permanent location, a gray day is exactly what is needed. Weed pulling, hoeing, draining the fish pond and mending the crack are good ways of spending a good gray day. That is, if you have an aptitude for such matters—and the season is spring.

In the subdued light and quiet calm, the arms of Morpheus may reach out and try to snatch us up. And sometimes they take us. Gray days are drowsy days. They are days meant for speculation on projects we aim to do some other day. They are the contrast of fair mornings and cloudless skies and shafts of sunlight piercing bough and branch. They are symbolic of existence itself, where the bitter and the sweet, the gay and the sad, the fair and the foul find their places in the pattern of events. Each serves its purpose.

Brighter days are more appreciated after dark days. Happiness is never so keenly felt as after an era of heartache and tears. There must be night if we would truly welcome the dawn.

In the throes of grief, the seemingly insignificant takes on significance. Such little things—the precious keepsakes to which we cling: a valentine, a pressed petunia, an old straw hat.

Worthless, that's what the world would say— "just trivial trash that sentiment clutches to the heart." And so they are—to others. But that's because they cannot know. They cannot see the radiance that encircles those humble items that once had a place in the life of our loved one. We pick them up.

Reverently, we pick up an old worn volume of verse, a scrap of paper with a grocery list jotted thereon, a half-used package of Burpee's tomato seed.

Strangers would give not a single copper for these mementoes of ours. And yet, all the earth's gold cannot equal the value that we place upon them. In that moment in which we clasp some

17

simple possession of his in our hand—in that moment, we seem to hear the old familiar voice:

"You know what? The fish frogs are calling tonight. Spring has come!"

They resurrect that which has gone.

The little intimate belongings bring back the days of laughter; neighbors coming over to sit with us on the porch; Papa coming in from the garden with the first mess of roasting ears.

They have lingered, these cherished bits. These and memories.

Not everyone feels thus. Not everyone can gather comfort from things closely connected with those so dear. To some they mean anguish. They mean yearning and heartbreak and tears. There are those who put away all the photographs, the knick-knacks upon the mantel, their loved one's favorite chair. They cannot bear the sight of these reminders. But for everyone who shoves all of the past into the closet and bolts the door, there are a million others who find solace in plain and simple objects. The fountain pen upon the desk; Henry Drummond's *Greatest Thing in the World* on the bedside table; the lawnmower sitting in a corner of the workshop. They speak a message. Each of these inanimate articles speaks of the one who used to handle them. In their own individual way, they tell of his love of reading; his habit of making marginal notes; of mowing the lawn when the day was young and the dewdrops still clung to every fresh, green blade.

And now, because I am surrounded by these things that belonged to Papa, he seems so near. Just in the other room, maybe. Or just stepped out to see if the mail has come. Or gone to dust the roses. That's all.

Just away for a moment, then he will be back.

In their company, in the company of these things which have

made up our everyday lives, our lives seem to go on together. It is easier that way.

Papa found it so.

When Mamma went away, he cherished every flower she had planted. He gathered the acorns from her scarlet oak tree and sent them all over the country—to be planted in memory of her.

He didn't run away.

He didn't hide every last reminder to save himself sorrow. He looked upon her oil paintings, her hand-painted china, her bed of Elegans lilies as a challenge—a challenge to carry on as she would have had him do.

And he did.

Little things . . . or pieces of a life. That's what they are. All different shapes and sizes and having to do with all the various departments of living—these things that belonged to Papa. Put together, they show a man's love for his work, his home, his family. And put together, they provide something tangible to steady the steps of those who are left behind, when the path is dark and steep. Thankful am I for the little things.

Their presence brightens the passing moments.

And one by one they come—the moments.

And the fact that they come singly is a blessing of no small measure. Thus it is, we can inch our way along.

Suddenly faced with a changed way of life, it is hard to find answers to every phase of our situation all at once. And it is in attempting to map out the entire course into the future that we weaken and weep.

So often, I think of the Londoner lost in a fog one dark winter night. He realized that he was on a road on which there were regularly spaced street lights. However, he couldn't see any distance ahead. And so he ceased trying. Instead, he let his gaze reach out no farther than the one small glimmer of the nearest light. With his eyes fastened on this faint glow, he set out in that specific direction. Once he was there, he sought out the next light. And again he let that be his goal . . . until at last he had found his way through the fog.

It is a story that offers solace for any problem.

If we refuse to think past this moment, or this day—we can make it. And finally, we will be able to look back and see how far we have come.

Because anniversaries come.

When you are a child, the only anniversaries you are aware of are Christmas and your own birthday. These are wonderful occasions and you look forward to them—counting the days until their arrival. But after a while, after you have lived a sum of years, other anniversaries begin to appear. Some of these are happy. Some are great, smothering mountains of sorrow that rise up year after year.

We see both kinds coming.

And even before they arrive, we find ourselves enveloped in remembering countless little incidents and events.

One of the first dates I heard mentioned at our house with annual regularity was September 29. Sometime during the day, Mamma would say to Papa, or Papa would say to Mamma:

"Do you remember five minutes to four [such and such number of] years ago today?"

Happy smiles would follow and warm embracing. I came to learn that at five minutes to four on the afternoon of September 29, 1909, Reverend Robert D. Licklider, minister of the 31st Street Baptist Church, pronounced my mother and father man and wife. A happy anniversary. But there were others.

There was March 17.

Year after year, usually at the breakfast table, Mamma or Papa would recall a March 17 of years back: "We were coming back from Mother's funeral (Papa's mother) and we got caught in the St. Patrick's Day parade. Do you remember?"

There was December 7, when the first little grandson was drowned.

And now more recently, there has been another date.

They say that time heals, that given a few years, the worst wounds mend. I don't know. We might think so at times. But the strains of a song are heard—"Asleep in the Deep" or "Can't You Hear Me Callin', Caroline" or "In the Garden"—and all of the life that is past wells up in vivid recollection. On Sunday evenings the whole family used to gather together, with Papa standing at the piano, singing—a soft, sweet basso.

There is no forgetting.

Neither is anyone sole possessor of certain significant dates—etched everlasting on thought. All who have lived any length of time have anniversaries that are enshrined in little niches of remembrance. They continue to come, the anniversaries. We wonder how we shall spend them, the difficult days.

Alone at the window, in the company of a row of green house plants, I try to decide.

Attention is attracted to a fresh new leaf which has just opened on the Angel Leaf begonia. It is hard to realize that this big, wide leaf has sprung from the little brown casing which clings to one point of the new leaf.

Here is life. And here is the husk.

No one can doubt that the new life—the big, broad leaf—is many times more grand, more satisfying, a more abundant fulfillment than the little wisp of a casing that once held it.

After a while the wisp will drop away—down to the earth to be swallowed up. And no one will grieve, nor will anyone remember the day when it falls off. Everyone will just look at the lovely leaf and rejoice in its release, in its free and prolific expression of all that is good and beautiful.

Here was a message. Here was a comforting illustration to lift the heart; in a measure, to help make a sad anniversary less sad.

Later that very night, I listened to the ticking of the big grandfather clock. And, as the pendulum swung back and forth, its insistent message reverberated through the silence of the house:

"One year . . . one year . . . one year!"

As if I could forget. As if I could forget that day—one year ago.

I thought of the begonia leaf. But still there were memories that were alive and new. They lay like the dew on the hours of the day. Through the morning. Through the noonday. Through the early hours of the evening. And now in the darkness, I listen to the clock's rhythmic reminder:

"One year . . . one year . . . one year!"

And my heart cries out in disbelief. Oh no, it is not true! So much time has not fled since last his warm hands touched my cheeks, and his lips pressed a kiss against my forehead. It isn't true.

But the clock insists: "One year . . . one year . . . one year."

But I tell you he was with me. I heard his call from the garden. When the crocus first peeped above the frozen earth, and when the wind sang through a hedge of lilacs—I heard him. I heard again the old joyous call:

"It's spring! It's spring! I have seen a robin!"

And all the while I sowed seeds and set out frail green plants in his garden, it seems he told me how. Just at the moment when I was trying to decide whether the butter beans should be planted eye-down or eye-up, I remembered. I remembered the way he had planted them. And that would be the answer. And it was just as if he had told me.

Then came summer and roses and long evenings on the front porch. People might say I was alone. But, ah no. I sat in the company of other evenings. Hot nights, when the flashing of glowworms beautified the darkness. Cooler nights, when the katydids sang from bush and tree and branch. We would talk. We would talk of gay things that had happened years before; we would tell of the antics of our two dogs, Freda and Muggie—and make plans to take a trip next year.

We would talk. And the happy things we said have come echoing back. Back. Back. Stories out of Papa's native mountains of the South—warm good humor. And excerpts from things we had read.

People are never very far from those they love when they have had a mutual fondness for the world's great literature and its music. The Bible. Shakespeare. Don't you know, I can still hear Papa's low resonant voice reading: "Come unto me, all ye that labor and are heavy-laden, and I will give you rest."

Just a word, just a song, just the bright hello of a friend whom we've both loved—the birds flying into the feeder that he made, to get their supper—all of this makes me feel his nearness.

Papa gone a year?

Ah, no! I tell you, dear grandfather clock, the sweet fragrance that exudes from a life well lived never ceases. 'Tis true.

And the clock ticks, ticks on. Only now, the message of the tick seems different. I listen. "He lives. He lives. He lives!"

3.

Happy Are The Poor

The phone jangled. Down went the tea towel I had been drying the supper dishes with and up came the receiver.

It's a moment often recalled. Because it was a new beginning, destined to provide a lively interest, and even a paycheck, for that time when all would be different.

Looking about the changed scene, there was to be that nagging question: "Where is everybody?" But there would also be a measure of comfort in work to do.

Said the lady on the other end of the line: "I am Charlene Tolle. And my husband and I want to thank you folk for the pork chops and applesauce."

"The what?"

That's the way it came about, this chance to work as a columnist on the Indianapolis *News*, the Great Hoosier Daily.

Of course, there were still earlier episodes that pointed a finger toward the future. One of these fragments of memory has to do with Aunt Myrtie, Mamma's sister. Once, when I was five years old, she was holding my hand and we were walking down her front walk toward the street. Suddenly Aunt Myrtie said:

"I want you to grow up and do what I always wanted to do. I want you to write."

When you are five years old, that doesn't mean a thing. However, several decades later you remember it. Just as you recall a fourth-grade teacher who insisted that you write your own poem for the school program. The rest of the kids were to choose a selection from a reader, but you were to write your own.

That's what happened. Later Mamma remembered, when I was twelve and battling the aftermath of polio. It was a challenging time for her, I can realize it now, trying to keep everyone cheered, when her own heart must have been so very saddened.

Once when I was trying to stand up in leg braces, I began to cry over the whole awful plight.

"What are you crying about?" Mamma said. Her head, capped with pretty red hair, was held high. She was even smiling. "You don't have anything to cry about. Now, if you had a wart on the end of your nose, that would be different. Then you would have a reason to cry."

We both began laughing, and the moment of anguish passed.

No doubt Mamma was trying to whet my interest in writers and their works when she would place books in my hands.

"Now," she would say, "while I'm washing the dishes, you read aloud to me. Here's a book of Edgar A. Guest's poems. And here's one of James Whitcomb Riley's."

It was the bright inspiring verses that she liked best. Sometimes, when I read a line that was particularly heart-lifting and happy, she would stop suddenly, take her hands out of the dishwater, and face me:

"Read it again, honey . . . that last sentence. You know, I could live on things like that, just thrive and live, without any food at all!"

So, gently, she nurtured a habit in her child, a habit of looking on the brighter side of things.

When interest lagged in reading, Mamma put the bread board across the arms of the wheelchair, plopped down a sheaf of paper and some sharpened pencils. "Now," she said, in all gaiety, "You write some rhymes. You can do it!"

Papa and Syd, my little brother, and Mamma and I had just come home from a ride one day. Mamma went out to get the mail, and came in, her face fairly beaming. She had a long white envelope in her hand. It was from the *Junior Home Magazine*.

Saying not a word, she had gathered up several of my childish attempts at writing verse and had sent them to that children's publication. They were directed to the department called "Up in Jo's Garret." This particular portion of the magazine bought occasional contributions from their youthful subscribers.

And this is exactly what they had done in my case. They had sent me a check for one dollar, the first money that I had ever earned, for a poem. It was called "Thanksgiving." It went like this:

> Thanksgiving is here,
> The best of the year,
> The time that brings,
> Good joy and cheer.

It was thrilling and it was wonderful to think that people were actually paid for nothing more than putting one word down after another. Henceforth, whenever any of my playmates, young cousins, or little neighbors did something outstanding—anything from winning an award for riding a pony to appearing in a ballet recital or skating competition—Mamma would always say:

27

"But, dear, you can write. You're going to make a life for yourself as a writer."

I was?

It was the one hope to which Mamma clung. And she had so little reason to hang onto this dream. For my own aspirations at ages twelve, thirteen, and fourteen were airy, fairy fantasies, balmy bubbles—like becoming a swimming star, or tennis champ, or dancing the whole night through with one handsome boy after another.

Fortunately or unfortunately, the grim impact of being lame never wholly registered. There was always a kind of pleasant supposition that, after a while, I would wake up and everything would be as it once was, before that cold swim in the icy waters of Fall Creek.

Now and then, as a teen-age scribe, I received other small token payments from editors for some little article or story. These always brought forth almost indescribable joy from the family, or, more especially, Mamma. Often, upon hearing of or experiencing some marked bit of gladness, she would manifest her delight by saying:

"I'm so happy I could lie down on the floor and roll."

It was typical of her effervescent way. But it remained merely an expression until some years later and another mail delivery. This time it was a check for fourteen dollars for a 1,400-word story about our family's move to the farm. I showed Mamma the check and the kind letter that came along. She read it and then she said:

"Now, you know I have threatened many times to get down on the floor and roll. Well, this time, I'm going to." And as quick as that, that plump little lady was down on our dining room rug, rolling over again and again.

I think I was sixteen years old when *Better Homes and Gar-*

dens magazine bought a little cooking item that I had sent them. By now, I was sending off all sorts of things to all sorts of magazines, hoping, hoping, hoping. Well, they accepted my offering, which just happened to deal with Mamma's family recipe for Kentucky Corn Dodgers. I was thrilled, utterly thrilled, to capture even this much attention from a well-known magazine. In a burst of wild exultation and joy, I said, "Oh, Mamma, thank you for having me!"

And Mamma, just as elated, said, "Thank you for coming!"

At times like this, whether I was to walk or never walk seemed of little consequence.

One finds out, sooner or later, that to truly enjoy whatever there is to eat, and sleep the sleep of the righteous, every man must sweat a little. The same goes for a woman. It is one of the problems of having a lot of money that there is no cause to mop one's own floors, wash one's own windows, or hustle out and get a job and go to work. It's unfortunate, but not many people are interested in toiling for a paycheck when there is no real need for money. So it is that those with ample funds wind up short in the long run. They miss the rush of energy that comes to those who must be up and at it. There is a stimulation in leaping into the shower and making ready for the day, when outside all is dark and the pink streaks of dawn are yet to come. The very urgency of having to get some place on time or run the risk of getting fired, clears the head, speeds up the cogs of thinking, helps one to feel awake and alive. It has to be so, if the difference between sleeping inside or out-of-doors depends on the dollars and cents of a salary.

Not having to exert one's self physically encourages the fatty tissues to pile up. Women are more inclined to stay slim if they are forced to climb a ladder and hang curtains, or scour walls.

Maybe even grab a hoe and stir up the earth in a peony bed. People alone, men or women, can do no better than to take on as much physical labor as their health will allow. Get the garden hose and wash the car, whitewash the back fence, or pick up a scythe and slash the weeds in the vacant lot next door.

And then when the newspaper arrives, turn to the classified column and see what is available in the way of a job. There are all kinds. By patience and persistence, it is possible to find something within any normally healthy person's capacities.

It can be an answer for those suddenly aware that their old way of life is gone. With the person or persons with whom one has shared one's life no longer around, the query repeats itself: "Where is everybody?"

Possibly, the people who are destined to fill one's future are those for whom there has never been much time in years past. Perhaps they are the people with whom we have always intended to become better acquainted, or whom we will eventually meet in the course of some new business venture. The saving grace of work has been a wholesome solution to more than one person who by a death in the family, or desertion, or divorce, or in the natural run of events has been left, a lone leaf on a barren tree.

It was on a bright, almost spring-like January day that Mamma left us. I was sitting by the bed, holding her hand—a hand that had helped stir up no less than a hundred thousand batches of hot biscuits, made sun-kissed strawberry preserves, rooted Patient Mary cuttings, stitched up school dresses and snagged little britches, minded both the bookkeeping in Papa's business and the household accounts, and, in all deftness and skill, did still life and landscape painting.

She painted many pictures, some of which won awards. She

read many books. And always she was encouraging the rest of us to go forward, to make use of our talents, to keep the level of our thinking and acting high, becoming, and respectable.

Mothers are such very important people.

Sometime thereafter, Papa was coming home from work. He stopped at the freezer locker in Carmel.

Later, proceeding down Smokey Road to our gate, he saw a tall, rather slimly built man striding along. Papa had seen him before, in his daily travels to and from town, but had simply driven on, never stopping. Today, for some reason, he pulled to a halt.

"Tell me," he called, "can I give you a lift?"

"Why, yes," said the man on foot, "that would be very nice."

The two men talked as they drove along. It turned out that Papa's passenger was a neighbor living not too far down the road. When the man stepped out of the car in front of his home, Papa said, "I have just been to the locker. Could you folks use some pork chops and applesauce?"

The incident went unmentioned. Indeed, the amazing results of that meeting came only after the telephone call from Charlene, the man's wife. Said the lady:

"My husband, Alec, enjoyed meeting your father. We would like to call on you all this next Sunday afternoon, if you are going to be home."

Still rather new at running a house and minding the social niceties, I did remember that Mamma always served refreshments when people came. That's how I happened to make an old-fashioned one-egg cake covered with maple frosting and showered with pecan halves.

The couple came. The four of us talked about life in our rural area—things like dealing with Cool Creek when the spring freshets came, and the fact that they were putting a fresh coat of white paint on the little church across from the cemetery. Some-time after the cake and coffee, conversation drifted into the sundry activities and occupations of the folks living thereabout. That's when it came to light that Alec Tolle was an editorial writer with the *News*. He had just alighted from the suburban bus that brought him home from work when Papa chanced along.

"I write, too," I said.

"You do?" said Mr. Tolle. "What do you write?"

Moments later, a scrapbook was laid on the gentleman's lap. In it, lined up page after page, were columns entitled, "The Lighthouse." They had been clipped from the Sheridan *News,* a weekly newspaper in our county, for which I had been doing the little feature for some twelve years.

With no other alternative, the kindly man began to turn through the book as the rest of us chatted away. Shortly thereafter, he very courteously handed the book back to me, saying not a word.

I wished that I had never mentioned it. After all they were just simple pieces about what went on around our house and the farm. I might have known they would not have been of any particular interest to an important man like an editorial writer on a big city paper.

Two days later, however, Mr. Tolle phoned. "You know," he began, "with the talking going on in the room around me Sunday, I could not read your stories. Tomorrow evening, after work, I would like to walk up and get your book and bring it home, so my wife and I can read your columns."

When Papa heard of the call, he said, "That's so nice of him to be interested in what my little lass is doing. Call him back, and tell him that I'll run 'em up in the car."

Several weeks passed. Then came the report from our neighbors. They had read the Lighthouse columns. Somehow, they thought the Indianapolis *News* might like to see them. So the scrapbook was now at the paper. Later came further word. The publisher, Mr. Eugene Pulliam, had taken the scrapbook home.

Papa was getting excited. As for my own reaction, I could not imagine that a newspaper of such ranking as the *News* could possibly have any interest in anything from my pen. So it was a surprise when Mr. Tolle, all unannounced, walked up to our house in the course of his afternoon "constitutional." The Indianapolis *News* would like to talk to the lady who wrote the Lighthouse column.

I missed Mamma that morning. I tried to dress the best I could—the salt-and-pepper shepherd's plaid suit, a tiny red hat, a little red silk scarf. There would have been a feeling of sureness and confidence if Mamma had just been on hand to look me over.

The meeting with the Editorial Director of the *News* was set for three in the afternoon. I would ride in with Papa in the morning as he went into town on business. There would be all day to browse, to shop, to wait.

At something around two in the afternoon, I sat down in a display chair in the furniture department of Block's Department Store. The arrangement of living room pieces was just in front of the elevators. From time to time, large groups of people would assemble, waiting for a car to go up or down. It was not long before I would be leaving to go to the *News* office.

Suddenly, out from a cluster of humanity that stood before one elevator door stepped a quick, rather hurried woman. She came near and bent down to speak. Said the lady:

33

"I just want to tell you how . . ." She hesitated, as if searching for the right word, "How . . . well, how well-groomed you look. How nice you look."

"Oh!" Utterly taken ,aback, and profoundly appreciative, I struggled for something to say. Finally, it sort of leaped out:

"Oh, thank you," I said. "Thank you so very much. Within just minutes, I will be going to the most important engagement of my life. And it helps . . ." I was near tears. "It helps so much to be told I look all right. So very much!"

The stranger shook off the thanks. "Well, it's just that I believe in telling people what I think." And she was off, swallowed up in the crowd that went down in the elevator.

I have never had any doubt that that woman was an angel Mamma had dispatched to me at the moment I needed her most.

At the front door of the old location of the *News*, 30 West Washington Street, waited Mr. Tolle. He greeted me in the manner so characteristic of the man, with gentle, reserved dignity. We walked together up to the Editorial offices. Came introductions to the various members of the staff, including the Editorial Director, and then the neighbor from across the road went on his way. It was time for the three o'clock bus. His part, his very important part in the pattern of events, was accomplished.

They were pleasant people. There was Jo Mohr, a vivacious young woman who was an editorial assistant. And there was Robbie Robinson, the *News* cartoonist, with a twinkle in his eye that evidenced an ability to see the funny side of things. And then there was John W. Hillman, a quiet man who would break into a smile suddenly and unexpectedly. He was the Editorial Director.

Said Mr. Hillman: "We'd like a thrice-weekly column that appeals to women for our Editorial page. You can write at home, and mail your columns in to us."

"But, Mr. Hillman, I've been writing just once a week for a country weekly. That's all I'm in the habit of doing."

There was a silence. And then the Director came up with a sage fact. "You never quit thinking, do you?"

"Well, no."

"Then write on just what you happen to be thinking about." It was an idea. The whole trick, of course, was to see that one's thoughts made fit reading. Little did I know that eventually there would be healing help in insistent deadlines. It is the only virtue in being poor, when time and circumstance leave one alone. You cannot very well pause to whimper and to grieve when there is a column to write and the postman is due in an hour.

4.

Listen! There Comes An Answer

It was in April that the first column appeared, the night of April 18. Papa could not wait for the newsboy to deliver the paper that evening, so he suggested that we drive into Broad Ripple and buy an early edition. Just north of the Monon Railroad tracks, we saw an Indianapolis *News* carrier. The car came to a halt.

"Got an extra?" Papa shouted.

"Yep!" said the little fellow.

Seconds later, we were parked at the edge of the road. Papa had the paper gaped open at the editorial page:

" 'My Window,' it says. Look!" He held the sheaf of pages over for me to see. "They have named it, 'My Window.' "

There it was, printed out in tall, beautiful letters at the top of the column. I repeated the words. But no sound came.

Papa swallowed hard. He started to read, and then he swallowed again. He looked up, and his eyes were glistening with tears. "Mommie would be so happy! Here, you read it. I can't. Read it aloud to me, as I drive."

37

The last paragraph had said, "Happiness is only complete when there is someone to share it.   . . .   "

But what do you do when there is no one near at hand to share it?

Now, years later, that was the problem.

A whippoorwill interrupted the thought. It was during that soft, gray interlude between sundown and darkness. And, for me, it was a wish fulfilled. Only days ago, a letter had come from a friend living in a remote area who had written about the woods and the wildlife in that vicinity. A single sentence in the letter uncapped a reservoir of recollection: "Last evening, a whippoor-will called." So long had it been since I had heard a whippoor-will—not since I was a little girl at our summer place in Brown County. These nocturnal birds do not usually frequent the heavi-ly populated areas of Indiana. They like the timber country. They like the quiet, the loneliness of dusk, miles away from civi-lized sounds.

I read the sentence again—and I wished that, even for one night, I could be where the whippoorwills called. Then it had happened, right here at home, on the fringe of a city of more than a half-million people.

Perhaps my correspondent, for so long so kind, had sent the whippoorwill—a memento, a bearer of serenity and peace. It was a fanciful and pleasant contemplation.

Miss Fluff, the white collie, and I had gone for a walk—our last one before the night bade the day farewell. We had just rounded the house where the Dorothy Perkins rose vines tum-bled over a white board fence when we heard that first whip-poorwill.

It came from the grove of young trees across the road. In rapid succession, he called again and again—whip-poor-will, whip-poor-will, whip-poor-will.   .   .   .

In spite of the brisk repetition of his name, the whippoorwill gives one a feeling of tranquillity. His very call drops the curtain on turmoil and unrest and brings a kind of soothing assurance that all is well. I simply cannot agree with naturalist John Burroughs. In one of his bird stories, he spoke of the whippoorwill's call as "a rude intrusion upon the stillness and harmony of the twilight hour." But apparently even Burroughs himself was not wholly in accord with his comment, because later, in describing the bird's song, he portrayed it as "a cry without music, insistent, loud, penetrating—and yet the ear welcomes it."

Once a neighbor of Burroughs' told of hearing a whippoorwill call two hundred times without stopping. Burroughs considered the story something of an exaggerated tale. However, the naturalist was soon able to tell a bigger one. Shortly thereafter, Burroughs counted 1,088 "wills," with only the slightest halt for breath. Once replenished, this same whippoorwill resumed his solo—this time running up 390 calls.

The call is a love song.

If the love song seems persistent, it's because the whippoorwill loves intently. Should you come upon a pair of birds (reddish brown, about the size of a robin), you will hear them clucking to each other in soft, endearing tones. Their nest is the forest floor. They quietly deposit two whitish spotted eggs on fallen dry leaves. Then, as the moon appears and the stars come out, the world listens as they say—"good night, good night!"

With sorrow, kin and friends inevitably get around to one specific suggestion—merely, to flee from the place of one's grief.

"Get away for a while," they urge. "Go somewhere. Meet new people. See new things. Just forget about home. Turn the key in the door and take off."

So blithely they offer their counsel, so easy they make it sound. In the grip of hurt one wonders if in truth there might be help in a trip—in going somewhere, anywhere. Maybe in going away and never coming back.

It's a possible solution that pops up, in fact, not only at the time of the loss of a loved one, but in myriad situations and frustrations. We're faced with making the old psychological decision—flight or fight. And momentarily it seems less complicated and the least effort to—run. Perhaps because we are tired, so tired.

Give us simplicity.

We ask for this and we ask for that. There is no end of wanting. One goal is won, then we set our eyes upon another. But after a while that which we want most is simplicity.

I have just been visiting with a couple who have come up the hard way. Henry peddled papers as a boy. He worked in a grocery after school. With younger brothers and sisters to help along, college was out of the question. At nineteen Henry was traveling over three states selling machine tools. Some place along the line, he met and married Mary. They began housekeeping in a couple of rented rooms. Mary worked in a department store and did the laundry at night. By hard work they would go places. They were sure of it. Someday Henry would have a share in the business. Someday, they would have a fine home. Someday, they would be rich.

Now, after thirty years, Henry and Mary find it hard to believe that "someday" has arrived. Henry has a share in the business. Henry and Mary own a fine home. As for being rich, they have all the money they need. More than they need, because

Henry is always looking around for a better investment. That's a worry he didn't use to have.

It came as a surprise to me to find a "For Sale" sign on Henry and Mary's home. I had no idea they were thinking of giving up their beautiful home—ten rooms of oriental rugs, mahogany, teakwood, and bric-a-brac. Lots of bric-a-brac. In late years, Henry and Mary have traveled a great deal. They have brought home rare laces, hand-wrought silver, wood carvings, statuary. Every room is laden with dust catchers. That's what Mary calls the mementoes. Henry agrees with her.

"We're tired," he says, "of so much responsibility. Once we were after security. Now, we're after simplicity."

So the big house is to be sold—the orientals, the mahogany, the teakwood, the bric-a-brac. It's all to go. Henry and Mary have leased a two-room apartment. Mary said: "We will have no more room than when we were first married. With fewer things, we hope to have more peace."

It's too bad. After thirty years spent in accumulating, Henry and Mary have come to the conclusion that having little is more satisfying than having much.

In this respect, the lower forms of life can teach us a lesson or two. The world outdoors is simple—beautifully simple. Ants and bees and night crawlers go about their respective chores—the major one being the acquiring of food. They make no special effort to out-do their neighbors, to make a name for themselves, to pack away enough groceries to last them for the rest of their lives. Their concern is more immediate. The ant and the bee are content if they have enough laid by for the coming winter. The night crawler lives it up as it turns up. Each has his small sphere of labor.

So it is with the tree, the fish in the stream, the birds of the air. A daffodil sends up a spear of green in the early spring. It blooms. It fades. It spends the winter sleeping, then rises to repeat the cycle. The little citizens of the out-of-doors have lived bountifully when they have fulfilled their simple and singular mission.

Not so with the human race. We are out to capture all that is to be had, never realizing that once our cup is full, we will weary of the weight.

"Simplicity, simplicity, simplicity," wrote Thoreau. "I say let your affairs be as two or three, and not a hundred or a thousand."

The call of the whippoorwill was a resounding reminder that one need not go looking for either simplicity or solace—yea, adventure. They can find you where you are. Had not a bird, rare in our area, suddenly appeared? To set forth on a search for comfort would be an endless journey, because anguish isn't something you slip off like a raincoat, then hang in the closet and go out and enjoy the sun.

Immanuel Kant, the German philosopher, was absolutely convinced that nothing was to be gained by traveling. Indeed, that wise man was violently opposed to the whole idea. Once a lady invited him to go riding. Kant accepted, thinking that they would take just a short run. Later, when the woman happened to mention that they were seven miles from home, the thinker was furious. He insisted that they return immediately. Angry that they should have wandered so far afield, Kant said hardly a word on the journey back. For thirty years thereafter, he refused to step foot inside a vehicle of any kind.

And yet, Kant lived fully, enjoying wide horizons of thought. He found endless interests in his own daily round in the environs of his house and neighborhood. For instance, there was his regular afternoon walk—a walk he took over the same route, at precisely the same time each day, from the time he was twenty years old until he was eighty. Apparently, his own mental pondering was all the company he ever desired or would allow on these methodical strolls. Perhaps it was during his some sixty years of hiking that he evolved his famous queries:

First, there was: "Who am I?" Secondly, "What am I?" Thirdly, "What can I do?" Fourthly, "What can I know?"

To the first and second queries Kant contrived a reply. It was as uncomplicated as this: "A wise man is the one who knows he does not know."

Kant figured this disposed of number one and number two— leaving only number three and number four. To the third question the only answer was: "What must I do?" There were four things, and four things only, that a man must do for his well-being, said Kant to Kant: (1) eat; (2) work; (3) associate with your kind; (4) rest.

As for the fourth query, "What can I know?": There were no boundaries to the mind. So why travel?

Sometime or other, there must be an adjustment to life without Mamma and life without Papa. To go away would be simply a postponement in establishing some new routine. Or, rather, to as nearly as possible go on with the activities and interests we had all followed.

Home and the kitchen, having folks in for, maybe, hot vegetable soup on a Saturday night, and taking note of the changing seasons yon side my window—this had been the pattern of affairs for so long. Momentarily, it seemed that the ultimate in simplicity and peace was not in doing something revolutionary and out of character, but in just following along that path I had known. Yes, and loved.

The quiet stillness that met me when I came back into the house shouted out the loneliness that awaits those left alone.

However, the whippoorwill had enlivened the last few minutes. Perhaps something else would happen after a while. Come what may, here was my little place on earth—and here I would try to piece together what was left.

And with that I got out the rolling pin and began rolling into crumbs a whole loaf of bread that had dried out. Already I was learning how little one person can eat—particularly, when he has no appetite. But the birds would like it. And by morning the feeder would be empty. It would be a terrible thing for them to come and find no breakfast. The rolling pin moved faster. And the crumbs piled up.

It was nice to feel needed—if only by a flock of wild birds looking for a hand-out. Who knows, the whippoorwill—my whippoorwill—might come. Who knows, he might wait around until the dawn and stop off for a bite.

Personalities are not restricted to persons. A few moments at the window observing the bird feeder and its callers are proof enough.

The winged customers who frequent the open-air cafeteria are decidedly different. Their demeanor is as varied as that of a crowd of spectators at a wrestling match. They are individuals flaunting their own brand of individuality. Indeed, they are characters. And from both sides of the track.

I'm thinking of a bluejay that bounces in, a dashing sort of guy who could very well be the advance agent for something. He is the fellow who gets in town, looks at the sports page and sees the announcement of a tag match, no holds barred—that's for him. Dapper, in a blue jacket and a black collar, he looks flashy—ah, sharp. But his good grooming is just feather deep. Inside, he is an uncouth, rough somebody who talks too much—and does it in a raucous, rasping voice.

Apparently uneducated and with little bringing up, he eyes his more cultured fellows, and sometimes makes a noble try at imitating them. But always he is the unsure chap at the dining table who does not know which fork to use for what. So, not knowing, he plunges in helter-skelter, get-out-of-my-way. He's all hog with no manners, shrieking forth his crude comment— usually with his mouth full. He's the chap who sits back of you at a wrestling exhibition, who enjoys an eye-gouging, and shouts: "Kill him! Kill the gol-darn, weak-kneed panty-waist!" There's a jay in every crowd. Usually, more than one.

Not so the cardinals—the ladies and gentlemen of birddom. They keep their poise and their composure. They stand back and wait. No unbecoming conduct with Mr. and Mrs. Cardinal (who, incidentally, do not sanction any change of partners. They mate for life). As to their dining habits, they eat at what you might call the second table: the crumbs and grain that fall from the feeder onto the ground. They are the shy type who, if they attended a wrestling match, would sit near the door. Then, should the opponents get too beastly and hammer too unmercifully with the hammer hold, they would quietly and unobtrusively get up and leave.

But now the chickadees and the titmice are the cordial middle-of-the-roaders. They are the sunny members of the audience who have an appreciation of physical prowess but want no man to cripple any other man. They have come to see a contest—fair and square. And they want all contenders to have just treatment. They are that sort, these sprightly individuals. They like everybody and everybody likes them. They wait their turn in the diner, standing shoulder to shoulder with starlings and whatever, grab a seed, then rush out to, maybe, hang head down on the trunk of a willow. It's a stunt comparable to standing about chatting and joking with passing friends and acquaintances.

There are lots of chickadees and titmice (or titmouses) in every wrestling crowd. They scrimp on the groceries to have a night's splurge, to compare ringside attendance with TV viewing, to see the best man win. And to enjoy cold pop and hot popcorn, and parrying punches.

True enough, out-of-the-ordinary diversion is just inches from my window. That mottled mass of temperaments, coming and going, is a regular parade of personalities. One long look and you are convinced. It takes all kinds of birds to make a world.

Reaching out for some tangible something to fill the empty days, I found myself again and again plunging into a heap of reference books in the search of an answer. Sometimes in the hunt for one thing, something else would turn up. Like: Why is the bluebird blue?

Right now, I have no idea whence the legend sprang, but the story went like this:

"The bluebirds were the only birds in the ark that continued to sing through the deluge of water. Neither gray-black clouds nor driving rains dampened their ecstatic delight. When at last the door of the ark was thrown open (after the dove had returned with an olive branch), it was a pair of bluebirds that flew out immediately.

"They headed straight up into the bright clearness above. However, the male bird pierced the blue sky first, with the result that he got a more generous coating of blue than his lady."

Other fascinating ideas came to light:

What about bird courtship? Do birds woo alike? Two robins feeding each other inspired the contemplation. 'Twas real touching to see robin goodfellow snatch a gnat from the air and then in all tenderness drop it into the mouth of his sweetheart.

But now, you take storks. They use another technique.

When they are of a mind to cuddle, a pair of storks will sidle up near each other and "twine their necks together in a loving embrace."

The albatross is more reserved. Mr. and Miss Albatross will meet on a lonely ocean island. With a good grip on his emotions, one will walk slowly up to the other. Suddenly, they will stop and, for a long time, look at the adored. And then they will make a long bow, and another, and another.

It's their way of smootching.

A bird in New Guinea called the fawn-breasted bowerbird makes quite a project of his love-making.

First, out of twigs and such, he builds a courtship house. And then he gathers assorted leaves and berries and hangs them about for decoration. With this done, he prances into the middle of his domicile and starts to dance, spreading his feathers like a real show-off. After a while, his luck holding out, he will grab a mate. With this done, the love nest is abandoned and they go off to build a home together.

What about feeding the birds in the summertime?

This is a matter for debate, but usually the birds win. Not that any of the winged clan need a donation during fair weather and growing times. After all, during spring and summer and early autumn the outdoor pantry is bulging with seeds, bugs, and other delicacies. But who wants to toss the remains of bread, cereal, peanut butter, melon rind, etc., into the garbage pail? And even a bird likes to get something without working and sweating for it. Incidentally, some of them may speak their thanks by hanging around later—maybe until the first snowflakes appear; maybe all winter.

47

It is well, too, to remember that every recognized restaurant includes a drink with their menu. For a bird, it is a must in the bill of fare when the weather is hot and water is scarce.

Possibly, a first move in adopting a changed manner of living was to give the immediate surroundings a searching look. Could it be that the pieces for building anew might sometimes be found on home territory?

What happens tomorrow could spring up from the seeds of today. Certainly, the view from my window was no less fascinating now than in time past—spring's first bee stumbling over a first dandelion bloom, the cottonwood clapping its leaves in a summer wind .   .   .   and now, a whippoorwill.

It was as if he had brought a message. Or, better still, an answer.

5.

Fifth Wheels

In between thinking out solutions to perplexing problems, the person left alone wakes up to an astounding fact. Namely, that he is not alone.

In the cozy compatibility of a family made up of a mother and father, sisters and brothers—and later a husband or wife, and still later one's children—one is likely to presume that the whole world is nestled into the warm presence of affectionate associations. One simply takes for granted that everybody has somebody—somebody who is on hand and cares whether they wake up in the morning with a runny nose, have had their feelings hurt, or need money for a new pair of shoes.

Yes, and who's happy when they are happy! Probably the nth degree of desolation comes when one has hit the jackpot, by way of some thrilling, wonderful event (maybe had his name drawn in the local shopping center and won a freezer), and there is nobody around to go soaring into the skies because of his good fortune.

Joy is sharing.

One can be sick alone, cry alone, but to be honestly and completely happy alone is something else. Usually, it is after such a

49

bout that the lone one pulls him or herself out of the dark depths of despair and takes a look around. And, maybe, for the first time becomes acutely aware of the plight of any number of others who are also alone.

They are everywhere, the soloists. For sundry reasons, people find themselves by themselves. And seldom by choice. By the turn of destiny, or the normal cycle of time, they are left on their own. Their numbers add up to startling figures. A survey by the Bureau of Statistics some few years ago revealed that there are in the United States 12,380,049 women who have never married. Widows and divorcees added up to 9,784,638. As for the men, the Bureau supplies these figures: single men: 15,412,733; widowers and those divorced, 3,532,343.

All of this is enough to convince us all that we are not alone in our situation of being alone. This realization is a good first step in the big building project of reconstructing a new life. Because it is inevitable. It must be done. Some things we cannot escape.

Of course, it may be a little late. Certainly nothing tears at the heart more painfully than to see people who have for so long shared their lives with others suddenly left alone. Maybe they have not made a major decision by themselves for years. And now, any number of vital matters concerning their future and well-being must be decided.

As agonizing as it is, now is the moment to admit that the past is past. If it is death that has put us on our own, we well know that life as it was will never be the same again. This may bring on a torrential rush of tears, but it will also help one to view one's circumstances more clearly and realistically.

Call it the second step in establishing a new pattern of living.

Having faced up to this stark truth, we can observe the manner in which other loners of our acquaintance have met the challenge. Need it be said that the 41,109,763 million men and women in the United States who are alone today have had to evolve some sort of plan by which to continue? How well they have succeeded is something we might well contemplate and consider.

Fifty years ago, a new independence began to creep into society. Prior to that time, it was customary for a lone mother or father, sister or brother, aunt or uncle—even destitute cousins or friends—to move in and become part of a family. Households were few that did not have an extra somebody occupying the featherbed in the back bedroom, or sleeping on the sanitary couch in the dining room. Most children grew up with a grandma in the house who always had a mound of mending in her lap, or who was chief dishwasher and maybe, now and then, made homemade yeast bread, coffee cake, and ginger cookies.

Or sometimes it was a grandpa who was real good at making sling shots. Or an old-maid aunt who had had an unhappy love affair in her youth and who was old and cross and took her teeth out at night.

These added members of the household were simply accepted as part of life's lot. To the community, they were something of objects of pity. And those whose hospitality they had accepted were regarded with admiration as shining examples of benevolence. Without doubt, such survivors from life's storms acted as a kind of sobering influence on growing youngsters—and their immediate elders as well. They were a constant reminder that if you lived long enough, you would get old.

In his latter years, the Hoosier poet James Whitcomb Riley, who had never married, began to worry about his lack of anchorage and solitary state. In the summer of 1893, he was spending an evening with a few friends in downtown Indianapolis when he announced: "I'm getting tired of this way of living—clean, dead tired, and fagged out, and sick of this whole Bohemian business."

Shortly thereafter, he came up from his home in Greenfield to visit his long-time friends Major Charles L. Holstein and his wife and family in Indianapolis. So many times previously, Riley had visited the Holsteins' comfortable old brick house at 528 Lockerbie Street. Time and again, he had accepted their dinner invitations. On this occasion, however, the parting was different. As the poet prepared to leave, he turned to the Major and said: "I'm never coming back again, except on one condition."

"What's this?" The Major was no little shocked. "And what may I ask is the condition?"

"That I come back as a boarder."

The Holsteins lost no time in extending a hand of welcome to their long-time poet friend to come under whatever conditions. And so it was that a lone man—not a poor man, but simply a lone soul yearning for the security of home—found refuge. Here on Lockerbie Street he spent the last years of his life. Here notables from the world over came to call on the renowned Riley. Though he never had title to the property, he enjoyed all the privileges of ownership. The hospitable Holsteins took care that their old friend felt completely at home. Historic accounts in no way indicate that either the Holsteins or Riley considered the poet a fifth wheel.

It still happens. But not so often as formerly. With women enjoying greater freedom and opportunity in business, with social security and pension plans, with commodious apartments designed for older people, and lush retirement homes, the person left alone today need not be cast on the mercy of others. That is, so far as home and the comforts of home are concerned. With even a small income, the lone individual may choose to make provisions for himself outside the realm of the family, if only in a rented room.

However, this is not an all-out declaration of independence. Shelter from the elements and food to eat are, of course, necessary. But the human spirit, to enjoy some measure of completeness, needs the association of kindred—if one be fortunate enough to have even distant relatives. There is a pleasant warmth in belonging, even if the ties are as distant as a fifty-fifth cousin. Someone with whom to share interests and memories, and with whom to spend Thanksgiving and Christmas and special days, marks the difference between being just a stray cat and a creature with background. Roots give a sense of stability and a reason for staying put rather than starting off down the road headed for Timbuktu.

Often, those who have been torn loose from one mooring can transfer their attentions and any assistance they can offer to some of the younger people in the family, who need everything from an occasional baby sitter to someone to water the geraniums and feed the dog when they are on vacation.

Stumbling along, trying to get a foothold in a new life, one now and then turns up some bright avenue of activity. Also, in a fresh awareness of others who have faced similar adjustments, one can pick up a few ideas on what not to do, and what to do.

Certainly, it was no small shock to hear that our friend Mrs. Oris Franklin (the name is changed but the facts are as stated) had applied for a job as a housekeeper. It had been no more than a year ago that Mrs. Franklin had come to live with her daughter Eleanor, wife of a prominent attorney in our community. With three children in the family, and not such a big house, it was decided that Mrs. Franklin would turn over all of her small savings to her daughter and son-in-law. By so doing they could arrange for a building contractor to put a dormer on their house, finish a bedroom in the attic, add an extra bathroom, and construct a stairway from the first floor.

Mrs. Franklin was then to live with the family, rent free, and take her meals with them. Being a very conscientious person, she could not help but feel under obligation for her food and this added expense to them. Having no income—her husband having died prior to the coming of social security—she determined to help her daughter Eleanor in every way possible with the house and with the children.

So it was that she took over the ironing and the mending. She also picked up after the children, helped them with their homework, told them stories before they went to sleep. With a full-time baby sitter in the house, Eleanor and Jim (that was her husband) began to take off on weekends together. Sometimes it was a flying trip to Chicago. Sometimes it was a cruise with friends. Sometimes it was simply to a cabin in Brown County where, as Jim said, they could hole in. After all, a change never hurt anybody, and of course Grandma was with the kids.

Everything went along very well for several months. And then, all of a sudden, Eleanor realized that the children were depending more and more on her mother. Seven-year-old Mike would get off the school bus and run straight into the house calling, "Grandmommie! Grandmommie! Guess what? You know that picture you watched me color last night? Teacher gave me a great big gold A on it!"

And somehow, twelve-year-old Linda could never find things. Maybe minutes before she would have to leave for school, she would cry out: "My ballpoint—where is it?"

Mrs. Franklin would hustle off to help.

It was the night that sixteen-year-old Kathy found a bright chintz pillow on the end of her bed that Eleanor exploded. Immediately upon seeing it, Kathy ran to the stairway leading up to the attic bedroom. "Oh, Grandmommie! Grandmommie, I love it!"

As it happened, Mrs. Franklin had simply taken a remnant of

chintz left over from curtains she had made for her own home years ago, and covered an old pillow that had been in Kathy's room.

At first it had been a kind of a smoldering something, with Eleanor spitting out quick, sharp sentences like escaping steam:

"How do you like being the boss of the house?" Eleanor said, over the top of a magazine she was reading. And later: "Mother, aren't you forgetting that these children are the responsibility of their daddy and me?"

But this time, leaping from the sofa almost like an enraged animal, Eleanor ran toward the stairway which Kathy and her grandmother were just then descending. Eleanor stood in the doorway:

"You know," she pointed up the stairs, "we remodeled the house so you could stay up there. You know that, don't you?"

"Mother!" Kathy looked at Eleanor, wide-eyed and unbelieving. "Whatever is the matter with you, talking to Grandmommie like that? Are you out of your mind?"

"See!" Eleanor spit steam again. "See what you have done . . . taken over the children!"

Mrs. Franklin grasped the railing leading up the stairway in order to hold herself upright. It seemed the strength was all gone from her legs. She opened her mouth to speak, but nothing came. She rubbed her free hand across her eyes as if to clear her vision. About then, Eleanor broke into violent sobbing and ran into the bedroom that she shared with Jim.

In fact, only moments later, that's where he found her, still crying, her head buried in a pillow. Jim sat down on the side of the bed, insisting that she tell him what was the trouble. After a while she sat up, red-eyed, the tears dripping off her cheeks and chin.

"It's Mother," she said between gasps, "she is trying to run things."

"What!" Jim got up off the bed. "Why, I should think you would be glad for some help!"

At that, Eleanor fell back on the bed again. "Oh, no! You, too! You, too!"

It was the next day that Mrs. Franklin applied for the job as a housekeeper in a home where there was a widower and his young daughter. Eleanor drove her mother over for the interview, and then took her back later to assume her new duties. It was just as Mrs. Franklin was hoisting her suitcase out of the back seat that Eleanor spoke:

"What are our friends going to say? What are they going to think?"

Mrs. Franklin still does not know how she did it. But she managed to smile. She even kissed Eleanor good-bye. "They will understand, honey. They will be smart enough to know what you and I had to learn. I mean, that no house is big enough for two women."

With Uncle Cleo it was different. It was just that from one day to the next, his whole life was changed. He had simply awakened one morning to find that his wife, Laura, had not awakened. Sometime in her sleep it had happened, and so quietly that Uncle Cleo, lying right alongside her, had never known.

It had not even been a year since Uncle Cleo had retired from his roofing business in New Haven, Connecticut, and moved to Akron. It was so that he and his wife could be near their only son and family. In fact, they had bought a small one-floor ranch house no more than a mile away from young Dan and his wife, Dell, and their two youngsters.

Shocked and hysterical at finding his lifeless Laura beside him, Uncle Cleo had leaped from the bed and rushed to the phone and called Dan. In moments, they were there. In all tenderness, both Dan and Dell gathered the old man in their arms. Trembling, he clung to them.

"What am I to do?" he sobbed. "I can't live without Laura! I don't want to live without Laura!"

Said Dell: "You're going home with us, Dad, right now. I'll run him home, Dan. And you get on the phone and make arrangements."

And that's the way it was. Uncle Cleo went to the home of his son and daughter-in-law.

"You be nice to Grandpa," Dell told the children. "Tell him you love him. And each of you give him a great big hug and kiss." And then Dell was off to be with Dan.

The next few days were a gray cloud for Uncle Cleo—a denseness through which he stumbled with only one light on the horizon: the goodness and the thoughtfulness of Dan and Dell and their children. He wondered what he could do for them to show his gratitude. He did not want to wait until he died. He wanted to show his appreciation right now.

And then one day, by chance, he heard Dan talking to Dell: "If we could only swing an airplane, that would make it so I could get over more territory, and still be back home every night."

Said Dell: "It does seem a shame to be a licensed pilot and have no plane of your own. What would one cost, dear?"

"Well," said Dan, "for the one I have in mind, it would be around twelve thousand dollars."

Uncle Cleo, in the next room, shining the kids' shoes for Sunday School, waited not a minute. "What's this I hear," he said, "about an airplane?"

"Dreaming, Dad, that's all," said Dan.

"Well, son, now is as good a time as any for you and Dell to discover that sometimes dreams come true. I want you to get right out and order that plane. The bill is on me."

"But, Dad!" Dell was near tears. "That's too much for you to do."

"Of course it is, Dad," said Dan. "It would wipe you out."

"But, Danny, what do I need with money? I have my pension. And you and Dell have given me a home. What more would an old man want?"

And so it was, Uncle Cleo wrote out a check for Dan's new airplane, and closed his savings account. But that was all right. There was the pension check. And that would give him enough. He could even have a new suit now and then, and a pair of shoes, and some change to buy things for the grandkids. When you were almost eighty you didn't need much, other than a roof over your head, and food, and a few folks to love you.

There was jubilation in the household for weeks, with everybody having their turn with Dan on an air jaunt—that is, everybody except Uncle Cleo. He insisted that he wasn't afraid to fly. It was just that he wanted always to keep one foot on the ground. And whenever he said that, there was a roar of laughter from the kids. Dan tried to figure it out in inches —how high you could get off the ground, and still keep one foot on the earth.

Uncle Cleo still recalls the merriment that went on—that is, before Dan came to his room one morning for a talk. He said he and Dell had an idea. They wanted to get Uncle Cleo a trailer, and park it out back so he could have his own quarters; he could get up when he wanted to, and go to bed when he wanted to, and fix what he would like to eat.

"Of course," added Dan, "Dell will run you to the laundromat, so you can do your shirts and sheets. . . ."

"But, son . . ." Uncle Cleo felt kind of dazed. It was all such a surprise, so unexpected. He began again. "But, son, I don't have the money to buy a trailer. They cost. And anyway, I'm happy. I hope I'm not bothering you all. Is it my pipe?" Uncle Cleo brightened up suddenly. "Is that it? Well, now, I don't have to have that old pipe. Your Mom was always trying to get me to give it up. You tell Dell that no good corncob is going out the window, as of right now. . . ." The old man got up and started to the window.

Dan stood up and took his dad by the arm. "No, Dad, don't do that. It's just that it would be better in lots of ways for you to have your own place . . . near us, but not with us . . ."

Dan had begun to stammer and grope for words. "I hope . . . I hope you understand, Dad. I . . . I hope this does not make you feel bad. I hope . . ."

Uncle Cleo shook his head. He wanted to say, "No, Danny. No, Danny, I don't feel bad. No, Danny, it's all right. I'll go. I'll do what you want me to do . . ." But nothing would come out. It was like when he woke up and found Laura gone to sleep . . . forever. It was like that. It was just like that.

Dan and Dell insisted that Uncle Cleo go along when they picked out the trailer. They wanted it to be just what he liked, his choice. Sure, they would pay for it: "But it is for you, Dad," said Dell. "And we want you to be happy."

"Happy." Uncle Cleo whispered the word to himself. Happy. Would he be happy in a trailer? Would Dan and Dell be happy with him in a trailer? Would the grandkiddies be happy? Well, if that is what it took for everybody to be happy, then by all means that was the thing to do.

And so he thought much. And he said hardly anything at all.

Really, as it turned out, it was sort of fun living in the bright little quarters, with the tiny stove and refrigerator. Dell and Dan even put a television set at one end of the small living room and had an extension telephone from their own home put beside his bed. For a while, Dell would send one of the children over with a tray at night just as the family was sitting down to their supper. Once or twice a week she would look in the door of the trailer.

"Going to the grocery, Dad," she would say. "Do you have a list made out?"

"A list?" said Uncle Cleo. "What kind of list?"

"Why, your groceries, Dad!" There was a hint of impatience in her voice that was uncomfortably noticeable.

"Oh, Dell, of course. Pardon me, child. Will I ever get used to running a house? Tell you what. I have a can of soup here, and a few crackers. Let's let things go at that right now. And next time you go to the store, I'll be ready. Who knows, I might even go with you."

The young woman, in pink flannel slacks and a white car coat, never answered. She just turned and walked out to the drive, and slid into the driver's seat of a station wagon.

It was on Sunday afternoon, just before Dell and Dan and the kids were to leave on their summer vacation, that Dan stepped into the living room of the trailer and dropped down on the sofa.

"Dad," he said, "we just can't leave you alone while we're away—no near neighbors around. There's a trailer court a couple of miles south of us, on State Road 9, nearer town. Dell and I want to have your trailer pulled down there before we leave."

"Oh now, son, don't you worry. I'll be fine. I can stay right here and watch over your house, and feed the dog and the cat."

But Dan was determined. Everything was going to be shut off

in the house. And they had already arranged to put the animals in a kennel.

"But," said Uncle Cleo, "you will bring the trailer and me back when you get home? Right?"

Dan was looking out a small window in the trailer. It was some time before he answered. "Let's see how you like it," he said. "After all, a trailer parked in the yard doesn't do a thing for the looks of our place."

Uncle Cleo was really quite surprised at how soon he adjusted to the new location. Dalton's Maple Grove Court was clean and neat, with dozens of elderly people like himself living in trailers. There were a sandwich bar and a coffee dispenser on the grounds. Every time he stopped in, he met somebody. One retired couple, a Bob and Mary Hines, even came over to Uncle Cleo's and spent an evening playing gin rummy.

Having gotten some brief insight into Dan's thinking concerning the trailer parked in his backyard, Uncle Cleo was all armed when the family came home: "Why, I'm just plain pleased, living here in this trailer court. Don't you young'uns try to talk me into going back. Nothing doing! I'm beginning to get acquainted, even making a few buddies."

There was really no need for the commentary; neither Dan nor Dell said a word about having the trailer brought back to their home.

If things had gone on as they were, Uncle Cleo might have worked up a gin rummy tournament. It's altogether possible. But several days went by and no one saw the old man. Somebody broke open his trailer door to investigate. Uncle Cleo was ill. Dan and Dell were notified. And Uncle Cleo was hustled off to a hospital.

For a long time, it looked as though he would not make it.

But he did. Only the doctor would not hear of his going back and living in the trailer, with no one to watch over him and prepare his meals.

Again Uncle Cleo argued: "I'll be fine. Why, I'm a good cook, Doc. You stop in someday, and I'll prove it to you. Cook you a kettle of ham and beans."

But once again it was a lost cause. Uncle Cleo's next address was a nursing home. At eighty years old, the possibility of the aged gentleman going back to his trailer seemed rather remote. So Dan and Dell sold the trailer and put Uncle Cleo's few possessions in a box and deposited them in their attic.

Having developed something of a knack, by this time, for adjusting to whatever came along, Uncle Cleo circulated around the nursing home. He found tasks for himself, things like reading the paper to folks who were blind, and walking down to the big R.F.D. box, and bringing in the mail. He even arranged with a nearby church to send a car over, so that anybody who was up and able could attend church Sunday morning.

The experiences of Uncle Cleo come to mind just now, what with a news item that appeared in the morning paper: The State Board, after an inspection of convalescent and nursing homes, has condemned the home in which Uncle Cleo has been living.

Upon reading the story, I dropped the paper in my lap. What now? Where will this old man, who so generously handed over his twelve thousand dollars for an airplane, go now?

It is a little late to start over.

6.

Women And Women

The present will forever be what the past has made. And the details of construction are a never-ending source of conversation.

No sooner had Beulah Everett arrived than we set about filling each other in on everything that had happened to each of us. These sudden spurts of recollection might take place any time—while one of us was slashing up cabbage for slaw; or carrying the waste paper out to the incinerator; or as we stood in the bedroom hall in our nightgowns, ready to retire to our respective rooms.

Memory is a spontaneous something that loves nothing better than someone to listen. And in relating the sundry and assorted events and experiences of our lives, Mrs. Everett and I became acquainted.

She had been a widow for a number of years. Her husband, George, had apparently been a good man, but had just never amassed much in the way of goods and chattels. They had had two children, a boy and a girl, who were both married now with grown children of their own. But for some reason Mrs. Everett preferred to be on her own—which seemed a rather spunky venture at seven decades and four.

During most of her married life she had lived with George's parents, who had had a big house in an old but respectable neighborhood—and whose rear yard backed right alongside Fall Creek.

When the parents died, Beulah Everett set about rearranging the house according to her own likes. George did not care. He was no sentimentalist. Neither was his wife. And anyway, for the first time since they were married, they would be head of their own domicile, with no kinfolks looking on—not even those staring out of a picture frame.

For Beulah Everett that was a first order of business.

One day after a hard downpour of rain, when our whole side yard looked like a lake, Mrs. Everett said, "It was after just such a storm as this that I sent Aunt Millie and Uncle Ted on a voyage."

"What do you mean 'voyage'?" I inquired.

Beulah Everett tossed back her curly head and laughed like a child who has put fishing worms in the teacher's gloves. "I mean, one night after George was in bed asleep . . .   no need to give him an aching conscience . . .   I got on a ladder and lifted his Aunt Millie and Uncle Ted off the wall—you know, their oil portraits—and carried them down to Fall Creek and tossed them in. Away they floated, face side up."

"Oh no, you wouldn't, Mrs. Everett. You wouldn't."

"Wouldn't I? Or, rather—didn't I? And please call me Beulah. I wish you would."

Periodically, from time to time, Beulah Everett was to make that request. Sometimes very pathetically. But somehow it didn't seem right, so soon to get so informal. Mamma and Papa's rigid rule that one should address their elders respectfully had too firm a hold . . .   even though saucy little Mrs. Everett certainly did not behave like an elder.

It was only when her hearing aid acted up and failed to func-

tion that her gaiety subsided. Once I chanced to see her swish-
ing away tears that were already trickling down her cheeks.
Startled at being seen at that instant, Mrs. Everett quickly
brightened:

"I have made a decision," she said. "You never can tell, some
handsome old man just might come along and ask me to marry
him. Now, don't make light of me. It could happen, and at seventy-four. Well, if it does, I'll say 'I will marry you on just one
condition—that you give me a garbage disposer. I'm not interested in any diamond ring. But I'll have to have a garbage disposer. That's definite . . . my final answer!' "

I had to admit they were a real convenience . . . and I
was glad our kitchen had such a handy device.

"Handy!" Beulah Everett repeated. "How I managed to live
up until now without one is beyond me."

The reason for the tears was never mentioned. And only shortly thereafter, Beulah Everett received a notice that she had been
accepted in a retirement home.

So soon again, the pattern of affairs was toppled. But a means
of procedure had been established. And with that settled, I
placed an advertisement in the paper:

Wanted: A gentle lady. . . .

Bettie Masters was from Nashville, Tennessee. She was sixty-
eight: a tiny, fragile woman with white hair neatly done, a soft
Southern accent, and a knack for tatting—with a shuttle, that
is. She was forever at it, making long stretches of lace for pillow
slips and dresser spreads. And if there was no other demand,
she would simply roll up the fruits of her efforts in a ball for
future use.

Mrs. Masters, like Mrs. Everett, was a widow. She had come
north to live with her brother and his wife. And then for one
reason or another had decided that she would like to move. She
had seen the ad for a gentle lady and decided her disposition

might fit that description. And so her brother offered to "carry" her and her suitcase to her newly chosen home. Or at least that was the way Mrs. Masters put it.

The word was always "carry." It was a taxi that "carried" her into town; good friends that "carried" her to church; and a bus headed south that was to "carry" her into another chapter of events.

Some three or four months after she arrived, Bettie Masters began to talk about going home for a visit—home being Nashville, Tennessee.

One day as she tatted she said, "I got a hankering to see my people. You never know about life—you know, what's waiting in the wings."

It was a fact you could not deny.

And so a week later, Mrs. Masters took her suitcase, got on a southbound bus, and left. "I'll be back," she said. "Probably in about ten days. I'll write you."

In no more than twenty-four hours, there was a telephone call. It was the brother's wife. Bettie Masters was seriously ill. Just before the bus got into Nashville, she had suffered a stroke and had been removed from the bus and taken to a hospital.

Apparently, the only thing permanent was change.

Louise and Syd were concerned. "You just cannot stay by yourself," said Louise. "We would worry. Cynthia and Bruce can take turns and come down after school and stay all night with you. They will love doing that."

Cynthia, 11, and Bruce, 6, were a lively variation. Conversation took a sudden shift. After all, the talk of elderly ladies doesn't exactly compare with the discussions of youngsters.

With Bruce it was model airplanes; and with Cynthia it was piano lessons, and Brownies, and learning to swim.

The school bus passed at seven-thirty A.M., Monday through Friday. So it was race, rush, and scurry, including breakfast, from six-thirty on. And sometimes seven on, if we had all sat up late the night before.

Bruce would leave television to play checkers, which seemed rather remarkable and unusual. But then he always won. Already, with only a half-dozen years to his credit, he could set up traps to capture my men, try my patience, and, incidentally, send thought into other fields.

And this was good. So gradually do those bereaved come to learn that the remedy for death is life.

It is the inevitable decision that one must make. Losing the love and companionship of someone dear, you can go to the grave and cry. Or you can figuratively crawl in a tomb of desolation, inertia, and memory. Or you can jump headlong into a seething upstir of interests—young ones, maybe, like a houseful of children. Not that there were that many. It just seemed that way.

Said Cynthia, after school one day as she sat on a stool in the kitchen eating a jelly sandwich: "I wish that there were some girls my age living around here."

It was the grievous blow destined to come. An aunt three times as old could not possibly substitute for young fun, despite fudge-making; serving as bass on piano duets; playing tick-tacktoe, and reading Louisa M. Alcott's *Little Women* aloud. I might have known.

"Well now, we could import some. You could even have a party."

"Oh, Mimi!" Cynthia sprang from the stool and spun around on her toes. "Could I, Mimi?" And then suddenly she stopped still, her hands outstretched in a kind of pleading fashion: "Could I have a slumber party?"

"Why . . . why . . ." This didn't seem too impossible. "Why, yes. That would be nice. A slumber party."

"Oh, I love you! I love you! I love you!" Once again she was spinning, this time on her heels, her auburn hair flying out from her face and the full skirt of her gingham dress whipping around in swirls. "I'll call Karen, and Susan, and Peggy, and April."

"So we are to have a convention of cousins," I said.

But Cynthia was already at the telephone dialing.

They came the following Saturday morning. However, for one reason or another, only two could make it. There was Peggy, twelve, with flaming red hair and a quick bubbling kind of laughter that would break forth for the least reason at all.

And then there was April, who was not quite eleven and who showed her exuberance by cartwheels and handsprings. And if the mood demanded, she would go into the more graceful movements of the ballet. Whether there was music to do it by did not seem to matter. It was the mood.

As for Cynthia, she exuded vocally . . . any song that momentarily expressed what she was feeling. Indeed, she was singing when the girls arrived. She was practicing Hoagy Carmichael's "Little Old Lady" for the Parent-Teachers Festival in which she was to appear on a program the following week.

"They're here! They're here!" She tore through the house, sliding a couple of times on small rugs, and almost tripping before she got to the door.

I got up from the piano seat where I had been playing her accompaniment and followed after her. It seemed the door sort of burst open, and the two young guests catapulted into the room.

Peggy had a bright green flowered robe over one arm, an overnight bag in the other, and a swimming suit dangling from her neck—having put her head through the arm holes. April was equally laden, only differently. She was wearing a play suit and carrying a dress on a hanger, with a roll of sheet music gripped under that arm, and a hat box in the other hand.

"Hi, Cyndy, hi!" cried Peggy. "You did ask me for a month, didn't you? I look like I'd have enough to last that long."

Everybody was laughing. But over it all I heard April saying, "Howdy-do, pretty thing! You're awful sweet to have us. Isn't she, Peg? Isn't she sweet?"

This time there were squeals. Cynthia was holding Peggy's swimming suit and was steering her by the head through the house with April close behind. They all three started toward me.

"Why, Mimi!" they shouted.

"We think this is great!" said Peggy.

"Magnificent!" said April.

"Fun!" said Cynthia. And they were off—half gallop and half canter.

"Straight east and turn to the right," I said, "to the big bedroom. Cynthia will show you where to put your things."

"Stop it!" shouted Peggy. "You're pulling my head off."

It seemed a good time to slip out and pick the daily crop of nasturtiums. After all, it was only ten in the morning. And we would just have a picnic lunch today. Before going to bed the night before I had made a big bowl of potato salad and the girls would probably like to fix hot dogs on the grill.

The garden seemed all silence and stillness after the clamor inside. Miss Fluff, the white collie, was beside me. "Why, how come?" I said. "Why don't you stay with the girls?"

Just then, a rabbit came through the fence from the adjoining meadow, and Miss Fluff took off. This did not promise to be a dull day.

I dropped down on the grass beside the bed of nasturtiums. The flowers, newly opened, had a look of freshness; the stems snapped off crisply. And there was a clean, good fragrance. I buried my face in the bouquet. It was interesting the way they were made . . . a unique sort of design. I counted the petals.

69

Three upper ones and three lower ones, and a couple of sort of fringed, fan-like affairs. The leaves were different, too—rather like an umbrella.

There was a loud whoop from the front yard, and Cynthia and April came racing around the house. They were in their swimming suits and were dripping wet and shrieking and squealing. "Peggy turned the hose on us!" Cynthia shouted.

"What did you do to her?"

The answer was quickly evident. Peggy rounded the corner, her red hair dripping and her wet suit clinging tightly to her young body. "Where did they go?" she called out.

"You mean Cynthia and April?"

"Yes . . . yes." She was laughing that bright dancing sort of laugh. "Look, Mimi, what they did to me!"

I had forgotten how amazingly capable children are of entertaining themselves. Came the question, however: was this getting a little too rambunctious?

"Yoo-hoo, Cynthia!" I called again. "Cynthia!"

"Yes, Mimi."

"Let's everybody get out of those wet swimming suits and into dry clothes. There is going to be an Aggravation Game in ten minutes over there under the willow tree—with prizes. Bring out the board and the marbles."

It was a long time, maybe three times ten minutes before the youngsters returned in dry shorts and blouses but with wet hair. Shortly after the game was under way, I went into the house to organize the picnic lunch.

There were to be hot dogs, potato salad, sugared apples on a stick, and chocolate chip cookies. I reached into the cupboard to get the platter of cookies. But they were gone. Neither plate nor cookies were anywhere to be seen.

It was late, maybe midnight or after, before the lively chatter in the big bedroom had subsided, and finally ceased altogether. I could hear the radio going, so I slipped in very quietly to turn it off. The bed lamp and the ceiling lights were still burning. But neither radio nor lights seemed to disturb the three girls stretched out full length on the bed. On top of the covers lay April's ballet slippers. And beside the slippers lay a book of riddles; and beside the book, a plate on which lay one chocolate chip cookie. Apparently all the rest were gone—gone to a good cause. Indeed, what better reason could any woman have for baking than feeding a flock of hungry kids? And for utmost enjoyment they should, by all means, be able to snitch them.

There in the blazing light of the bedroom, with the radio squawking, and the three young faces placid in sleep, all signs indicated that the party wasn't exactly dull.

After Sunday dinner, the girls insisted that the kitchen was their territory. Off with me. I wondered what was up. It couldn't be anything too bad—not in the kitchen piled with dirty dishes, skillets and stew kettles.

Sometime around four in the afternoon, I awakened from a nap in the porch glider and sauntered out into the rear portion of the house to see what was going on. There in the center of the breakfast room table was a heaping mound of cookies with a note tucked down in one corner. I picked it up. Scribbled thereon was this message:

WE THOT WE'D LEAVE YOU AS GOOD AS BEFORE
GOBBLED UP YOURS. HOPE YOU LIKE 'EM.
SIGNED: PENNY, APRIL, CYNDY

Glancing out the window, I saw them. They were in the side yard, sitting in the grass under the willow tree, a plate of cookies on the ground beside them. Munching one of those cookies they had made for me, I went out to join the youngsters.

71

April had a daisy in her hand, pulling one petal and then another: "He loves me," she said. "He loves me not. He loves me. He loves me not. He loves—"

Just then they looked up. "Hi!" they cried.

"Came to get your recipe," I said. "What's the name of them, anyway? They're wonderful."

"Hermits," said Cynthia. "Don't you know, I learned how to make them in 4-H?"

It was a detail that had been forgotten. Probably because I had not wanted to remember. When children get so they can make their own cookies you are not nearly so important anymore.

Before nightfall, Peggy's mother and dad came for her; and April's folks came. And all of a sudden we were alone.

Cynthia said, "The girls wanted to clean up the kitchen, but I wouldn't let them. I told them that I wanted to do it. It would be my way of saying 'Thank you to Mimi' for having the party."

This was too much. The tides of time were rushing away more swiftly than was pleasant. It was sort of terrifying. For a long moment I waited for the words by which to respond to the child's sweetness. And then in a kind of wild rush it leaped out: "You little old scallywag, you! Git! And quit growing up so fast!"

It wasn't at all what I wanted to say. But right then it expressed what was going on inside.

Not long afterward, Miss Grace came. Her name was really Grace Alecia Dailey, a tall, spare woman who had always worked as a domestic. But some few weeks later she quietly mentioned the fact that wherever she had worked the people had called her Miss Grace. Even though she was an elder by many years, this seemed respectful enough. And Miss Grace seemed happy enough until the suburban transit company took off the Sunday buses.

With church her only diversion, she felt compelled to make a change. She explained one morning as she ran the dust mop around the edges of the rug:

"But now listen," she said in all earnestness, "I'm not going to leave you until you get someone else."

Once again, the "Wanted, a gentle lady" advertisement went into the paper. Applicants were asked to write to an address box number. Thirty answers came—that many women considered themselves of mild manners and serene temperament.

The replies were interesting; lone and drifting souls, looking for an anchorage. One letter stood out from all the rest: "I was a housewife for more than twenty-five years, or until my husband died. Since then I have been doing clerical work and living in an apartment . . . I have no children.

"But now the store at which I have been working has been sold, and the new owners consider me too old to continue with them. My social security will not be enough to support me in the apartment in which I have been living. So I'll just have to make a move.

"As to my cooking, it's always suited me. As to how you would like it, that's something else. . . ."

There was something forthright about what the woman had to say. Maybe not particularly gentle, but nevertheless appealing. After reading the whole heap of letters, I placed this one on top.

7.

Perennial Planning

Tulips will bloom this spring because there were those who planted bulbs this past autumn, and other autumns.

They dug deep (three times the depth of the bulb), and into the hole they placed something closely resembling big brown onions. Then they covered them up and piled on some mulch. Then came the winter. And the ice. And the cold sweep of wind that piled up towering mounds of snow on the newly made flower bed.

However, he who planted never doubted that one day the sun would shine warm and green sprouts would shoot up from the hard brown earth; spears of leaves would come, buds appear, and after a while tulip blossoms. He never doubted.

That's what you call faith.

Questions arise; decisions must be made, and often there is no one around who can tell us what to do. So it is, we reach out for an answer. This reaching out, or prayer, can happen when you are out on the back porch ironing the kitchen curtains. Or maybe when your hands are in the dishwater. Or perhaps when, in the yearning for a solution, one has slid out of a chair onto one's knees, and buried one's head in the footstool.

75

In a communion with God comes a peace. Indeed, in the very earnestness of one's prayers, one can become still inside. It's a quiet and a rest not unlike the Psalmist must have known when he said: "Thou compasseth my path . . ."

It's the voice of faith.

Today grew old. The sunset came. Later there was night. No one has promised us the morning, nor has anyone prepared and signed a paper to assure us of tomorrow's dawn.

Yet, who is troubled, or uneasy, or afraid? No one gives it a thought.

After the night has come the day. For eons, it has been so. It is beyond our range of speculation to presume things would ever change.

That's what you call faith.

We realize that it would be a terrible thing if the law of gravity would suddenly give way, and everybody would be hurled into the wide expanse of limitless space. Terrible!

Trees. Houses. Buildings. Bridges. Every object, along with every living creature, to be tossed from its place of habitation into the indefinable nowhere. But because this friendly force has functioned quite smoothly and efficiently for, lo, this long, long time, we confidently go our way, believing that all will continue well and good.

That being the case, one might as well make plans for repainting the house this summer, getting the new tomato plants started, and making a slip cover for the sofa in the front room.

That's what you call faith.

I remember a spring.

The leaves on the trees were half-grown. Indeed, the foliage was dense enough to hide a bird's nest. But a late frost came and sent the leaves to the ground. "What would happen now?" we asked. "A leafless summer?"

But the trees were not discouraged.

They simply tried again. They had faith enough to believe that maybe next time they would win.

Hope is a robin—a brave first robin that arrives on a cold February morning.

Hope is a patch of grass that shows up between two bigger patches of melting snow.

Hope is a bit of blue sky midst gray-black storm clouds.

Hope is the one small star that makes any night less dark.

Hope is a whisper that says: "Tomorrow will be better."

Hope is a fierce, earnest belief that there is something worthwhile, something fine, something decent, in the one all others condemn.

Hope is the invisible impetus that lays on the whip, that fires drive; that somehow keeps up a relentless striving when, really, if we would only admit it, there isn't a ghost of a chance.

Hope is the child in us all, the eager wishing for that which any adult should know is wholly beyond our reach.

Hope is the whistle that steps up the courage of the whistler.

Hope is the morning, fresh and new, bearing in its arms the opportunities of a day—time to forgive, to try again, to say, "I'm sorry."

Hope is work. The spirit rallies when mind and hands are busy. Completely involved in even simple things, like washing dishes, shoveling snow, or mopping up muddy tracks off the floor, a future which may at the moment look all black can take on a brighter glow.

Hope is fun—the ingenious talent of finding a laugh in a problem that has us bent low beneath the load. Mirth has a way of lightening matters—and of making the heaviest cross a little less heavy.

Hope is love—the warm, sweet assurance that we are not alone. The tender, sympathetic support of just one person we honestly feel sincerely cares is enough to send us marching straight into the face of the foe.

Hope is a word, a verse, a line that pounds upon our conscious thought; maybe some ancient saw that puts starch in our spine, something like: "Nothing ventured, nothing gained."

Hope is a seed. Out of so small a thing as a seed can spring an apple tree whose boughs of blossoms will, in the process of affairs, supply—well, who knows how many apple pies? So we learn that in the apparently insignificant facets of a situation may lie the potentials of triumph.

Hope is the quiet sister of anticipation.

Hope waits around—sure that eventually every good dream comes true. Anticipation dashes here and there, all glee and elation, exuberantly confident that the race is all but won.

Hope could be a leprechaun, or a sprite, or an elf. Sure, ah, sure, it's a little something that nobody can see. Yet nobody can doubt when it's around.

Hope is one of the few real things of life that can exist without roots, foundation—or reason. You can't touch it; neither can you always explain it. But often the hope in some dogged, determined, never-say-die someone is all that keeps a tribe of people battling.

Hope is the long vigil at a sickbed—the stalwart certainty that no prayer goes unanswered.

Hope is the last member of a fighting front to admit defeat—and even then hope rejoices in certain promises.

It was Joyce Kilmer, the poet who penned the poem "Trees," who once wrote to a friend:

"I pray that I can love more. Really, nothing else matters. If I can just love enough, I know all else will fade away."

It was during World War I, and Kilmer was seeing suffering, and bloodshed, and death.

He could sense in love a panacea for the turmoil and the confusion and the horror of war.

All of this is a reminder of the Sign of Namasta in the Indian culture. In certain portions of India, the natives do not shake hands. Rather, as they approach one another, each holds his or her hands in a prayer-like posture.

The gesture says: "I see God in you."

The Christophers in one issue of their publication, *Christopher Notes,* carried this item: "Just before her opening song each time she appeared at the Metropolitan Opera House, a famous singer used to pause for a brief moment and whisper to the audience: 'I love you! I love you!' "

It was the star's own special way of remembering an important fact: She was not there to heap glory upon herself, but to bring happiness and enjoyment to all those people out there. The story was used in connection with an article entitled "How to Become an Effective Speaker." Apparently, a first requisite in the matter of becoming a successful orator is to have a warm spot in your heart for your audience.

By having a really sincere love for one's listeners, a speaker can talk with feeling and conviction. As the Christophers say: "Whether your audience consists of one or two persons, a dozen or a thousand, you will more readily win both their hearts and their heads if the chief objective is to enrich their lives—rather than merely further your own interests."

It is rather interesting to consider the many relatives of that one word—"love."

It is like a color that, shining through a prism, breaks itself up into various shades.

Courtesy is a phase of love. So is kindness. So is thoughtfulness. So is compassion. So is honesty. So is friendship. So is devotion. So is esteem. So is forgiveness. So is loyalty. So is unselfishness.

It shows itself in a thousand different ways. Yea, more than that.

Only right now we think of that which is not love, rather than that which is.

Love does not tell on itself. It does not say: "You know, I once went without an overcoat to buy you a new dress for the Junior Prom." Neither does it divulge the fact that "for years we have had to support Aunt Lola."

The Christophers and the man Paul think alike. There is faith, and there is hope, and there is love. And the latter is greater than the other two.

However, with the separation from someone we hold dear, the very immensity of love in our lives can create a very wide and aching void.

Immediately we are confronted with two alternatives: We can continue to yearn for that which has forever gone; or we can find what happiness we can with what we have. Indeed, in times of great loneliness and loss, we are made to see that for every need there is an answer.

Not the same answer, of course, that we once knew. But still a solace.

For instance, if there is no one about to serve as our sounding board, maybe we can talk to someone afar, by letter. Like this:

Dear Melinda,

There is nothing so important as having some one person to whom we can tell all. Because every now and then a host of thoughts well up within. Sometimes they are questions. Sometimes they are pleas. But they demand an airing.

And it is good to have someone like you, Melinda, to whom I can confide.

This sudden realization dawned upon me just moments ago. I was out by the white board fence, looking at the moonvines that have woven a wall of green—a wall studded with blossoms as white as new snow.

My heart leaped at the sight—the luxuriant growth, the sturdy vines, the miracle of so much substance springing from so small a seed. It was almost awesome. It was certainly inspiring.

I was thankful to find joy in so common a spectacle as moonvine trailing over a garden fence.

Wasn't it William Blake who talked about the world in a grain of sand, and heaven in a wild flower? You know, I think he had something there. Maybe, the key to contentment.

Long ago you and I talked in such a way. Everyone was taking a vacation, and we felt that we couldn't afford it, so we decided to look for excitement in simple things.

"Sure," we said, "it would be wonderful to go to California, to Alaska, or even visit the Louvre. But it is also wonderful to watch a spider draw out silver thread from his minute form and spin a home of gauze.

"There is a pleasant feel in a sunbeam resting gently on your cheek. It is warm. And it is tender."

And we wanted always to have an awareness of the sun—and the white clouds that drifted aimlessly across the arched heavens of blue—and the wind that sang through the cottonwood at night—and the rain that tapped on our window.

I have thought of it often, with additions now and then. Such as: Let us never be too involved with such a round of mundane matters that we fail to notice and appreciate the moods of nature. The gray days. The bright days. The wild array of colors that makes a sunset.

Or be too busy to stop and look and say "Thank you" for the work of the Master Hand.

Maybe you will smile at this, but, Melinda, let us never get too grown up; never be completely adult.

We want always to like warm cookies right from the oven—each with a raisin on top. We want always to be able to sit on the back step with some of the neighbor's young ones and talk fairies.

And in the spring, when some of the kids knock on our door with the first dandelion—we want to be just as thrilled with the discovery as they are.

Nothing is gained in losing the wide-eyed wonderment of childhood. Who wants to have seen everything, done everything, met everybody of note? Not us.

We want always to have something wonderful to look forward to tomorrow.

Some day we want to see a mountain capped with snow. Some day we want to watch a sailboat skim lightly over blue waters. Some day we . . . ah, there is no end to wanting. But that, too, is simple and exciting. Our world is small. We both realize that, Melinda.

But so long as we live on the edge of life and get only occasional sips of a part of all that exists, we are not likely to get bored.

That is reason enough to be grateful for having little. Thanks, dear, for listening. 'Bye now.

Later, a strange light flooded the room. I knew it had been raining. But I had not noticed that our portion of the world—all shimmering in a sudden shower—had taken on the unusual and rosy hue of the sunset.

The folks across the way, who ordinarily have a white house, now had a pink one. For a better view, I hurried to the wider, longer picture window. There it was: a gentle curve of pale pink and green, and darker rose, with a ribbon of sunshine. For some reason the sight of a rainbow puts a brighter outlook on one's whole circumstances and situation. For some reason, you feel happy suddenly.

According to Greek mythology, Iris was the golden-winged messenger of Juno, the queen of the heavens.

Queen Juno needed help. It was her assigned duty to preside over marriages and births. So Iris lent her aid by carrying word from Queen Juno to earth. And the path Iris trod, to and from the earth, was the rainbow.

Beholding that colorful arch in the sky, one sort of mentally kneels in wonder and in reverence. Various thinkers, from time to time, have contributed their conclusions about rainbows. There was Marco Antonio de Dominis, and Descartes, and Sir Isaac Newton. One reference work devotes more than a half-page to explaining the geometrical theory of a rainbow. But who wants to get technical with things like laughter and spring, sun and rain—and rainbows?

It's enough to know that the magic happens when behind you is the sun, and before you is the rain.

It has been explained. Let's see. The sunlight is composed of seven colors: violet, indigo, blue, green, yellow, orange, red. Every color has a wavelength. Really.

All these varying wavelengths of color enter the various raindrops and disperse themselves into the spectrum that we call the rainbow. Only no two people see the same rainbow, because no two pairs of eyes are in precisely the same spot.

The colorful bow in the heavens has different names in many of the countries around the globe. Some people know it as "The little window in the sky." Others call it "The bridge of the Holy Spirit." And still others, "The girdle of God."

I was wondering how far it would be to the end of the rainbow when our genial little newscarrier, Bill Porter, arrived with the evening paper.

Said Bill: "Several blocks back, when I first saw the rainbow, it looked like the end was right over your house."

Well . . . And all this time I had thought the pot of gold was way off yonder.

8.

Pride And Empty Rooms

She came—the woman who had answered the advertisement for a "gentle lady." Only when does gentleness cease, and blunt, unadorned honesty begin?

It was on a softly warm May evening, when the Maiden Blush apple tree was in bloom, that Hilda arrived. She was a plumpish little woman, somewhere between 65 and 70. Her letter had not been misleading. She was as straightforward and outspoken as her application. Faced with compulsory retirement and naught save social security to live on, she had an urgent need to find a place where she could manage on a small income.

Once we had each stated our needs and our capabilities, Hilda declared herself: "Now, I don't know you, and you don't know me. And I don't know whether I will like you. And you don't know whether you will like me. So I'm going to pay another month's rent on my apartment.

"And then I would like to come out here and stay with you for that month. In thirty days, we should know whether or not we want to go ahead."

And with that, she turned to the lady who had driven her out, indicating she was ready to go. It seemed fair enough. And with no one risking anything. For her room and board, Hilda would cook and wash dishes for the two of us. The main thing, of course, was that she would be on hand, a living presence, someone to talk with and to share the days.

Susie, faithful Susie, who had done the cleaning for so many years, would continue to come as always.

Sometime later, maybe a couple of months, Hilda said she would like to make a confession: "You know, the night I first came to talk with you?"

I nodded.

"Well, when we were going out to get in the car, I looked up and saw that tree full of apple blossoms. They were so waxy and fragile-looking in the darkness, and there was such a sweet delicate fragrance—I couldn't resist. I reached up and broke off a branch to take back to the apartment."

Anybody else would have never mentioned it. But, typical of her nature, Hilda could not stand to have the record read any way other than clean and right. Deceit, either then or now, has no abiding place in the sturdy character of this honest, generous soul. So I soon learned that if you wanted the truth, you could ask Hilda. And if you didn't want the truth, you might hear it anyway, simply for the reason that she thought you should know.

The day she arrived for her trial stint, she came loaded with parcels and assorted containers of foodstuffs. There were some choice cuts of beef that she felt would be nice to have on hand in the freezer—expensive things like sirloin and T-bone—and veal cutlets. She brought a bowl of just-made potato salad, garnished with hard-boiled eggs and bright bits of red pimiento.

"Here," she said, "is a quart of homemade mayonnaise . . . real mayonnaise. That stuff you buy is not fit to eat. I make my own."

Sundry and assorted delicacies came out of Hilda's basket. There were several cartons of strawberries, and new peas, and green beans. She explained that she had been to the City Market earlier in the day.

"I go several times a week," said this lady beautiful. "I have been for over forty years."

It was easy to see that living so luxuriantly might have its problems for anyone relegated to no other income than social security. The future looked lavish. Conversation took off at high speed, and in no time at all Hilda and I had synopses of each other's past. Indeed, for anyone so given to briskness, she was amazingly sympathetic toward my occasional tears. And my sentiment in hanging on to any little bit of anything that had belonged to Mamma and Papa.

Said Hilda: "I'm going to get you a new cookie sheet next time I'm downtown, and then we'll pitch that old charred-up one of yours out."

"Why, you're not going to do anything of the sort, Hilda. That's Mamma's cookie sheet. It's the one that she always used when she baked biscuits. I wouldn't give it up for anything!"

And Hilda, who liked the latest, shiniest, brightest, most up-to-date gadgets in cooking wear, simply shook her head. This time in quiet resignation. After all, she had lost her dear ones, too . . . her mother, and her father, and her sister, and her husband . . . and more recently, a young nephew whom she had adored.

Her husband, Frank, had been with the Pennsylvania Railroad until his death some twelve years before. It wasn't long before I felt as though I knew Frank. Hilda's recollections of him were that vivid.

Suddenly, in the middle of one morning when I was between the bedroom and the kitchen, Hilda reminded me that our thirty-day test run was up. It was a detail that had not come into my mind. In fact, this new set-up had become so comfortable and so accepted that it seemed impossible there should be any question about its endurance.

"Now, I like you," said Hilda, "and I would like to stay . . . that is, if you want me to, only not under our present arrangement."

This was a shock. It had seemed all right to me. I felt a little hurt and annoyed. "What's wrong with things as they are?"

"Just this," Hilda replied. "I don't like feeling tied down. When I go downtown, I don't want to look at my watch and see that it's time to hurry home and get supper. I did that all the years I was married, but I don't want to do it anymore."

"But supper is not that important. I don't care when we eat. Anyhow, I can get my own supper. That's what I had been doing before you came. Don't forget that I love to cook."

"But that was not the deal." There was a determined look in the face of my new friend. "Now," she said, "this is what I would like to do." She paused as if she were taking on strength and stamina for a steep climb.

"I wish you would give some serious thought to the very least rent you could take for that little room!"

"Rent? What do you mean, rent?"

"That's what I mean. I want to stay. And I'll do what I can to help you. But I want to be free to do what I want to, when I want to."

"Well, you can do that, and not have to pay any rent." All this seemed nonsensical and foolish so far as I was concerned.

"No." Hilda was emphatic. "I'd feel obligated."

And that's the way it happened. It was either go ahead on Hilda's terms or this lady-come-lately would be going back to the apartment she had waiting, going back to figure out some other solution to her retirement situation. Rather than have this happen, the lady got her way . . . all the way. She was not only to pay rent; she insisted that she do her own laundry and buy her own groceries.

The modest rental she felt that she could pay would allow for the whole carefully outlined program, all of which would leave her free and without obligation. And with that culmination arose a side issue that was to result in one hassle after another between us.

She never stopped. She was busy all the time. "Hilda," I would shout, "you're not going to wash those dishes. You have been on your feet for hours. Now, you go sit down and I'll do it."

"Will you hush!" She talked to me as though I were a stepchild. "For years I have been used to keeping house. Are you going to deprive me of the joy of doing what I have been accustomed to do? And . . . love to do?"

And Susie, off in the next room washing woodwork, would begin to laugh. She knew we were at it again. "We have arguments at our house," said the cleaning woman, who was a mother of twelve, "but not like that. Nobody wants to do the dishes!"

It is odd how taking money from someone living in your house puts an entirely different complexion on matters. By the mere action of currency being laid across one's palm for the use of a bed and the room in which it is situated, one becomes a landlady.

Somehow the word had a not too pleasant ring.

But neither had the thought of having this refreshingly frank woman step out of my life.

Both of us made mention of the proposed arrangement with the kinfolk and friends who chanced by at this time. Everybody was of one accord: If paying rent would be more suitable to

Hilda, let her pay rent. After all, she had a right to preserve her dignity. And, certainly, to pay one's way carried more dignity than to work for one's room and board.

So much for Hilda's dignity. But what about mine? This business of being a landlady. . . .

There seemed to be no other alternative than to gulp down the offer. And, as elegantly as possible, assume the new role. In my mind's eye, I envisioned the composite picture of a woman who ran a rooming house: Probably buxom, with a scrubbed, stern face; either with a broom in her hand, or waggling a bony finger under the nose of a roomer who was two weeks behind on his or her rent.

It was enough to make you slightly sick to your stomach.

But over and above all of this was the hope that, in spite of Hilda's decision, our comfortable and happy association would continue as before.

Only days later, we set up the bridge table on the front porch and got out the Scrabble Board.

Said Hilda: "I have a good word. And it's a double, too, but how do you spell it?"

"Spell what?"

"Syrup."

I grabbed the dictionary and looked under *si*, then *se*, then *su*. . . . Hilda jumped up. "I know what I'll do." She hurried into the kitchen and came back with a bottle in which a brown liquid swished about. Plastered across the front was a label reading: MAPLE SYRUP.

It was one way to find out how to spell "syrup."

Sometime thereafter, during one of our nightly games, there was a phone call. And as suddenly as that came a query which tossed another quandary into our now placid plan of existence.

A gentle, soft little voice spoke: "Would you rent a room to a widow lady? I'm quiet and stay to myself, don't smoke, or anything like that . . ."

A neighbor had told a neighbor, and she had told her aunt, and then the aunt had told her sister—so it is that the word gets around that Miss or Mrs. So-and-So takes in roomers.

The whole idea was something to make one cringe. And yet, this little voice was so pathetically asking for just someplace that she could be to herself. And not bother anybody. Living with relatives, a young couple and their family of little stair-step young ones, was getting increasingly difficult.

"I'd be content," said the small voice, "with a very small, out-of-the-way room."

I thought of the big, cheerfully furnished master bedroom that Papa had occupied until the last, and which had been closed up for many months. With a reason to clear out and dispose of things, maybe there would come the courage to tackle that sad chore. I hung up with the suggestion that the lady call back the next day. And with that I returned to the Scrabble game and Hilda. Only, we did not resume our playing for a long while. We talked about the lady who wanted so much to get to herself.

"She sounded very nice," I said. "You know, refined and educated."

"Well, to tell you the truth," said Hilda, "I have thought all the way along that you were being very foolish in not getting into your father's room and giving his things away. There is no point in putting off such a matter. After all, there are people in this world who could use those clothes."

She hesitated. Somehow I knew what was coming. So I was not at all surprised when she added: "And you have already found out there is at least one soul around that really needs that room."

Clara Collester looked exactly like she sounded on the telephone—tiny and frail, so retiring that she acted frightened. Hilda and I tried to get her to play Scrabble with us. But she insisted that she liked to stay to herself.

It was plain to see that she was shy, and overly careful that she did not infringe on anyone's territory. One day when she whisked up her breakfast dishes and pushed them back on the cabinet to make way for Hilda's morning cereal bowl and tea cup, Hilda spoke out:

"Will you come back here to this sink and finish what you were doing?!"

"Well," explained Clara, "I would have been in your way."

"You were here working before I finished eating," said Hilda. "And anyhow, you pay more rent than I do, and that gives you special privileges—like pushing me out."

Everybody laughed. However, Clara found some excuse to go to her room. And her dishes waited until the kitchen was empty and nobody would be in the least inconvenienced while she occupied the spot at the sink.

That November, on a Sunday afternoon, we all went to the fairgrounds to see the ice show. As we each crawled into the back seat of the taxi, the driver chuckled and said: "What do I have here, the Three Musketeers?"

In that moment the warm bond that had begun to grow among the three of us took on strength and tenderness. We were a trio of waifs who had found each other and were less lonely because we were together. And now, even sharing a Sunday afternoon outing.

"Yes," said Clara, "that's us, the three muskrats!"

Hilda looked at me and winked. We were making headway. Clara was beginning to feel as though she belonged.

The feeling grew. More and more, we would all eat our meals

together. "The dinner is on me today. I'm fixing a pot of corn and beans," Hilda said one afternoon.

"Well, then let me make a salad," said Clara.

"Who wants a pumpkin pie?" I asked.

"Not me," Hilda answered, lightning quick. "I hate pumpkin pie. Couldn't you just as easy make it apple?"

Apparently it was just a very bad cold that put Clara into bed early the next summer. Hilda kept telling her that she should do something for it.

"I am," said little Clara in a voice that was even smaller than usual. And she smeared more salve on her throat and chest. And insisted on coming out into the kitchen to fix herself a cup of coffee.

"You get back into that bed," said Hilda sharply, "or I am going to turn you over my knee."

Three or four days later, you could hear Clara breathing clear into the next room. Her face was flushed. Hilda and I both asked if we could call her doctor. We asked her again and again. Could we call her family, those young people with whom she had been living?

Finally, one morning we slipped out to the extension phone in the back of the house and called the niece. In just a little while, the girl and her mother arrived. They gathered up little Clara, wrapping her from head to toe in blankets, and hustled her off to a doctor. The doctor in turn hustled her off to the hospital, and within a week Clara was gone.

Hilda went out into the yard and picked an armload of purple iris and daisies and lemon lilies. Somehow we thought Clara would like that, flowers from our own garden.

At the funeral, Clara's family and friends came up to Hilda and me, one after another. A tall, gray-haired man from out of town who said he was Clara's cousin was one of the ones who spoke with us:

"I want to thank you," he said, "for the happiness you gave Clara. She so enjoyed living with you folks at your home. She wrote to my wife and me, telling us about you all. She said she felt as though she were back in college again, living in the girls' dorm."

And then there was the niece and her family: "You know even as ill as Aunt Clara was while she was in the hospital, she kept asking the doctor when she would be well enough to leave the hospital and go back to her 'own' home."

As I remembered Clara's earnest plea in the beginning for "just a little room where she could be to herself," the expression, her "own home," took on vast and momentous meaning. However, momentarily it was not sadness but more of a joyous thankfulness that fragile little Clara had at last realized her greatest hope in living apart from her family, in quarters for which she was paying.

Apparently it had taken her almost seventy years to pull away from all ties and strike out alone. It was a goal achieved, even though it was of short duration.

Somehow it put a changed outlook on renting rooms. Sharing one's home was more than providing someone with a bed to sleep in, a chair in which to sit, the use of a stove and a refrigerator. Sharing a home could be supplying someone with a measure of independence, the feeling of being a person in one's own right. It was a place where one could go inside and close the door, and make no excuses for not coming out to supper. It was one small nook in the world in which one could drop pretensions, relax, and be at ease. Quietly embraced within the four walls, one could be sure one was not imposing one's presence or any obligations upon anyone else.

A room off to oneself was not just a roof, a shelter from the rain, from the cold or the darkness of night. It could be a refuge from quarreling adults, screaming kids, and the wear and tear of a job. It could be a way-station between stops, a tomb wherein to rest, until courage and hope and resolve staged a resurrection.

And in return for all of this the landlady or the landlord received more than just so many dollars per week for the rent of a room. There are intangible results and compensations.

For anyone somewhat out of the mainstream of life and living, simply coming into contact with people of different backgrounds and interests is enriching. In the close proximity of dwelling within the same house, even though in different areas, one has a chance to observe the wide variety of habits, viewpoints and customs that mark one individual from another. From the ensuing conversation comes a glimpse into other fields of thinking and activity. And by way of this, those people who are somewhat shut in learn a little about what goes on outside their scope. There is a stimulation in having a young business girl rush home at noon on Saturday, jump into her tennis togs and take off for the nearest park.

Incidentally, in the process, a stodgy old landlady whose chief exercise is reaching out and turning the television on and off can learn something about tennis.

And the very fact that someone is making her home at one's house, at least for the time being, gives one a wonderful sense of being important and needed. It offers another reason for keeping the taxes paid and the roof in shape, and for planting a row of zinnias along the back fence. It is not enough to do all of these things just for oneself.

Indeed, renting a room can even make it possible for a lone woman, or even a man, to continue living in his own home.

Renting a room can be better than hiring a full-time housekeeper or companion.

Often older persons do not need around-the-clock attention. They do not want it. In fact, they get irked at having somebody around all the time. It infringes on their freedom and privacy. But if there is a roomer on hand at night, one who can note the health and well-being of the homeowner before leaving each morning and again upon arriving in the evening, often that is sufficient.

The children and the grandchildren are satisfied, and do not feel that they are sidestepping their duty.

It is simply healthy and wholesome for there to be coming and going at a house, for there to be more than one person abiding in a dwelling.

Sometimes a roomer, or even two roomers, is an answer.

With a change in attitude, it was not long after little Clara's room was cleared and had had a general housecleaning that an advertisement went into the paper. And so began a series of experiences having to do with people who rented the room that had originally belonged to Papa. And most of the experiences have been good.

Sometimes, in the course of events, men and women of high caliber, brilliant and talented, need a place to live just temporarily. Any number of those delightful souls have chanced our way. For instance, there were Phil and Elizabeth, just married. Phil was an architectural engineering professor at one of our big state universities. He had taken a summer job with an architectural firm in our city, and he and his young wife needed a home from the middle of June until school started the last of September.

Having that happy bride and groom in the house put a radiance over the whole place. We even had a Scrabble tournament, between Hilda and me and Phil and Elizabeth. There were long talks on the front porch in the moonlight, with all of us telling our stories from the far away past to the present. Once during their stay, Phil had to make a quickie weekend trip to San Francisco. Before he left the Bay City, he called on the most elite and ultra-grand pastry shop in the town, and he flew back with a luscious variety of bake things for our breakfast the morning following his return.

The pleasant friendship continued after Phil and Elizabeth had gone back to their college job. In fact, when the university sent the couple to Formosa to assist in the opening of the architectural school at Formosa University, Phil and Elizabeth wrote and arranged to spend their last New Year's Eve in the United States before their departure with Hilda and me.

Upon their return to this country, they came to see us, bearing for us each a kimono from Formosa.

Elderly and retired Elmer Jarvis was almost a masculine double of little Clara . . . quiet, meek, broken-hearted over the recent death of his wife. At the time of a vacancy, his sister from South Carolina called to arrange for her and her brother to come and see the room. She was trying to get him settled before she went back to her home.

They came. Some of their friends came. And it was decided that Elmer should have the room. They even all pitched in and helped him move. The poor man was that frustrated and helpless. Once he was settled, the sister went her way. And Elmer set about becoming adjusted to life in a rented room. It was a great change from living in a beautiful big house of his own in one of the more exclusive areas of the city.

Trying to fill in the long hours, he offered to take Hilda to the grocery anytime she wanted to go. Hilda, not wanting to seem indifferent or unfriendly, accepted.

97

It had happened several times, the two of them taking off in the morning for the nearest shopping center. One day they returned shortly after noon bringing me a corned beef sandwich, a really luscious sandwich.

"Where did you get it?" I asked.

Hilda explained. She and Elmer had gone into a neighborhood cafe and had their lunch together—corned beef sandwiches and a couple of beers apiece.

"Beer!" I was horrified. "You mean, Hilda, you and Mr. Jarvis sat down in that cafe and drank beer together?"

"Why, yes. What's wrong with that?"

"What's wrong? What's wrong?" I was absolutely stunned. Two people living at my home had been out drinking beer in a neighborhood cafe. I felt like a fallen woman, running a nasty house.

"Mr. Jarvis!" I went to the door of the attached garage into which the old man had just driven his car. "Will you come here a moment?"

"Why, yes, ma'm."

Somewhat feeble, he clasped the frame of the door as he mounted the one step leading into the house. "You want me for something?"

"I do."

Mr. Jarvis sort of tottered as he approached. At the entrance to the kitchen he reached out and clasped the door knob to steady himself. He looked at me, a question on his face.

"Hilda tells me," I nodded toward Hilda, who was just putting a sheet of aluminum foil in the bottom of the oven, "that you two have been in town drinking beer together."

"Well," Elmer spoke low, "we got a sandwich and then got a couple of bottles to drink with it."

It was just all too awful to believe. Brought up by parents who had been brought up by parents before them, and still those before them, who had adhered to the strict old-time Baptist convictions of no card playing, no dancing, and no drinking, I felt as if disrepute had come upon the family name. After all, these people had come forth from the home Papa had so recently left.

There was a thick, grim silence in the room, with no noise save the crunching of aluminum foil as Hilda lined the lower segment of the oven.

Finally, the generations of stern forbearance and ancestral philosophy burst forth in one great cataract of feeling: "Can't you all see how utterly shameful and disgraceful it looks for a man and woman who happen to be rooming at the same house to be seen in a public place drinking together? Can't you see? Don't you agree that it's coarse, and vulgar, and . . . and common?"

Still nobody said anything. Mr. Jarvis continued to grip the door knob, and Hilda kept on with her foil. These people, older than Mamma and Papa would have been if they had been still living, had nothing to say. Probably because I did not wait long enough to give them a chance.

"All I can ask is that you all make up your minds. Either get your things together and move or give me some assurance that so long as you two live under this roof, you will never go out together and drink in a public restaurant where everybody that comes and goes can see you."

There was still that stunned stillness. However, those good, honest souls may have been chuckling inside at the tirade of such a straight-laced upstart.

Hilda, her oven finally done, raised up and settled both hands on her hips. "Well, quiet down. There was nothing wrong in it, but if that's the way you feel, why it will never happen again."

Poor Mr. Jarvis, looking pale, his lower lip quivering, managed to get out a couple of words: "No . . . no, more."

Perhaps if the events of the near future could have been foreseen, the incident would have been allowed to pass without comment. The elderly man never offered to take Hilda to the grocery again. Some weeks later he was out for a walk. Just outside our gate, Hilda looked out to see him clasping a road sign to keep from falling. She called me to the window to notice the way Mr. Jarvis was weaving from side to side.

"Hilda," I said, "you'd better go help him."

She did. She took Elmer Jarvis by the arm and slowly guided him back to the house. He couldn't make it alone. It was a long time before he would let us call his doctor. In fact, not until morning. The doctor's examination was brief. He asked to use the phone.

"Elmer has had a stroke. And I've got to get him into the hospital."

They left, the doctor and the old man, in the doctor's car. And so another chapter closed. From the hospital, Mr. Jarvis went into a nursing home. And from the nursing home, he moved on to that place afar where, who knows, no one may look askance on two old people in their seventies going out and cooling their aged throats with a few gulps of ice-cold beer.

The rent on a room never adds up to a lot of money. No one renting rooms ever got rich. But in coming into contact with a variety of people of varying ages and upbringings, you learn a lot. Not the least of which is compassion and tolerance.

When the heavenly records are laid open for inspection, it will not be Hilda and Mr. Jarvis who will be trying to explain and seek an understanding ear.

9.

To Reach A Star

Because not many of us are self-starters, the fire within is usually kindled by another, even the will to live.

Call it an incentive.

Physiology can tell you where to find the liver, the gall bladder, and the sacroiliac. But who can locate an incentive?

That's because it is not bone, or blood, or muscle. It is intangible—as weightless as a shadow. And yet it is as strong as hope, as sturdy as another's faith in you, and your forever love of them.

It's that invisible drive that keeps us at it when we are tired, indescribably tired, and momentarily would abandon all efforts, give up the struggle.

Only—incentive doesn't quit.

Pick up most any book. Note the foreword, or the acknowledgment, or the dedication. In all earnestness, the grateful author pays humble tribute to some blessed one who has supplied the important push.

Call it incentive.

Betty McDonald wrote, in her book, *The Egg and I,* "To my sister, Mary, who has always believed that I can do anything she puts her mind to."

Thomas Paine wrote, in his *Rights of Man*: "To George Washington, President of the United States of America . . . I present you a small treatise in defense of the principles of freedom which your exemplary virtue hath so eminently contributed to establish . . ."

Thus the motivating idea, the incentive behind Paine's classic work, is revealed.

Trace any achievement to its beginning, and you find an overwhelming desire to fulfill, at all costs, an ambition, an ideal.

There is a difference between anticipation and incentive. Anticipation merely looks forward to spring. Incentive has the gusto to get a spade and plant daffodils—to make the spring more beautiful.

Always, it takes an impelling force.

It is something you think about when the one you love is not on hand to encourage your efforts and build up your confidence.

Or when death leaves us floundering for some real reason why we should even try to go on. At such times, to recall the lives and experiences of others steadies our own course.

This occurred to me just today as I heard Carrie Jacobs Bond's immortal song, "A Perfect Day." Carrie Jacobs Bond, who composed more than six hundred songs, will no doubt forever remain one of the world's best-loved composers. She had little musical education. Hers was the natural gift given to the few. With her young husband, Frank, Carrie lived in a logging camp in northern Wisconsin. It was a healthy, happy life. And Carrie was happy. She sang as she went about her work. After baby Frederick's arrival, the songs were lullabies. After her husband's death, they were songs of longing—songs like "Just a-Wearyin' for You," "Parting," and "Shadows."

Penniless, she and little Frederick went to Chicago. Mrs. Bond obtained work. She did sewing. Sometimes in her spare time she painted china.

A woman for whom she worked heard her singing. The woman, inquiring as to the name of the song, learned that Mrs. Bond had written it. In fact, she learned that her seamstress had written many songs, none of which had ever been submitted to a publisher. The lady insisted that Mrs. Bond bundle up some manuscripts and send them to a publisher.

Carrie did.

The music firm bought eleven songs, sending her a check for $35.

The dressmaker was encouraged. Maybe she could sell more. She wrote more. But success was yet a rugged road ahead. By hard work she got there.

Her song "A Perfect Day" was written in Riverside, California. Mrs. Bond had gone with friends to view the sunset from the peak of Mt. Rubidoux. The whole occasion was heartwarming and wonderful.

Back at the Mission Inn, dressing for dinner, Mrs. Bond snatched up a pencil and paper. She wanted to express her appreciation to her friends in some out-of-the-ordinary manner.

There was no time for corrections, so she slipped the verse into her purse. At the dinner table that night, she read the poem aloud:

> "When you come to the end of a perfect day,
> And you sit alone with your thoughts,
> While the chimes ring out with a carol gay,
> For the joy that the day has brought. . . ."

Perhaps we should more duly regard the gift of a day, that period between dawn and dark.

It's a quantity of time handed to us with no strings attached. It's ours. We may do with it as we please. But success or failure hangs on the decision. It is rather awesome when you stop to think about it—the potential of a day. No one gets more. No one gets less. To each is allotted an equal portion of daylight. The management of our allotment is up to us. Ours is the decision for whom we will work. Ours to decide the use of the hours left over.

"But," says someone, "I have a family. I have a husband, and a home, and children. My time is not my own."

Ah, now, stop and remember. What occupies your life today was your decision on some other day. Maybe five, ten, even fifty years ago you decided to give your heart to the man you loved. The home and children, the meal-getting and dishwashing—they are the natural results of that decision.

Never doubt that it was a good one. The hand that rocks the cradle still rules the world. And the hand that rocks the cradle has days that are as gay and varied as the rainbow we so recently watched from our window.

There's laughter; there's the scream after a bumped nose; twenty-three gross of peanut butter and jelly sandwiches. One feels impelled to tell young mothers: "Enjoy it. It won't last. So soon it will be over." And you will awaken one day to a new life, a strange life. Most everyone, if he lives, is faced with that startling query: "Where is everybody?"

The days will be what we make them. They can be lonely days, days of remembering other days that are gone; or they can be days of usefulness, seeking and finding other avenues of interest.

Lacking someone to supply an incentive, we must give heed to those angel visitants—ideas.

Groping in the darkness, we can experience a burst of light. Out of some commonplace incident may come a sudden dawn—an inspiration. It can be the feel of rain upon your face, one sparrow hunting for a crumb, the rattle of a shutter on a windy night. Strange how common things can sometimes become uncommon. Strange how the mere memories of another day served as the springboard from which Carrie Jacobs Bond found words for a poem. Strange how the look of the sky, the sound of a cardinal, the scent of boiling coffee can cut the moorings and send thoughts soaring into clear, clear heights. Strange.

I think of it now.

The house is still. Across the floor lies a shaft of moonlight. It's a golden path over which fairies might skip lightly, or dreams take on dimensions and hue.

I look at it—and fancy turns capricious. Perchance . . . perchance the moon isn't a man at all. Perchance the moon is a lady. And that sweep of gold across the carpet is the filmy train of a gown worn by her majesty, the queen of the night.

Ah, hers is a warm and ingratiating presence that loosens the tongues of men—and sets pens on fire. Yet innumerable scribes have been moved to eloquence by less lofty matters than a slumbering world dripping in moonbeams.

Inspiration can be the child of very humble parents: Ralph Waldo Emerson once became quite enthusiastic over a worm. Robert Louis Stevenson wrote something of a classic on money. And Shakespeare actually spoke philosophically about a toothache.

One thing we know—that without inspiration no one can design a bridge, paint a masterpiece, or invent a new device to peel potatoes. Inspiration is a kind of key that unlocks a chamber of contemplation. Sometimes that key is nothing more than a chance comment—a word that lifts the veil and reveals a fresh horizon. Companioning with those who are not afraid to be different has its reward. To wander through the thought fields of another is to gather rich grain—food for your own hungry soul.

Now and then the seeing eye can even pick up what might seem, like manna, heaven-sent.

One day Michelangelo was in the supply yard of a builder. He came across a big chunk of misshapen marble. He went immediately to the man in charge: "Tell me, sir," he said, "what are you going to do with that unusual piece of marble?"

"Nothing," said the man. "It is useless."

"Ah, no," said Michelangelo. "It certainly is not useless. Send it around to my studio. There is an angel imprisoned within it, and I must set it free."

The mind breathes. It both exhales and inhales. From this and that—butterflies and sticks and stones, and an avenue of moonlight—it has its intake. From the place we are and the sundry happenings that surround us can come inspiration.

In time everyone comes to the realization that real satisfaction is best attained by being of service to others. The late Senator Walter F. George of Georgia once reiterated this truism. For almost thirty-five years, the Senator served continuously in the United States Senate. It would seem that that should comprise a fairly sizeable contribution to the welfare of his countrymen; however, the Senator felt differently. Said the gentleman:

"The one great, profound regret of my life is that I've been able to do so little good for mankind."

Men and women have thought along these lines for centuries. It was Stephen Grellet who first said: "I expect to pass though this world but once." Later Ellen H. Underwood put it into verse:

"The bread that bringeth strength I want to give,
The water pure that bids the thirsty live;
I want to help the fainting day by day;
I'm sure I shall not pass again this way."

Apparently, it is rather firmly established that our earthly tenure is a one-way pass. It is also rather firmly established that the most we can get out of the experience is the good we can put into another's experience. This being the case, the lot of us had better sit down and map out a course: What is the greatest avenue of usefulness? In what field of activity can an individual best benefit his fellow travelers? These are interesting questions. I asked them of a retired office worker. She was ready with an answer:

"The maximum of good that anyone could do," she said, "would be to provide even more large camps throughout the country where city children could go without cost. It would not be just a one-week or two-week stay. Children could stay the entire summer."

That was her solemn conviction. I asked another, my own grandfather. Said Grandpa: "There is no better way to help than through the ministry. Look at Billy Graham. Think of the thousands who have turned to Christianity because of his efforts."

It was a worthy observation. But the next person queried had another conclusion, just as sincere, just as definite. Said the lady: "The big need is to do more for older people, the ones who have been put on a shelf and forgotten. What about providing suitable employment for them, work within their capacities? It is a universal need."

The answers were revealing.

But in the matter of mapping out a new life, there seemed to be no specific blueprint—no one job that one could tackle and say: "This is the *summum bonum*, the supreme good."

Each person has a different concept of usefulness. He looks out from his own point of view and sees a need. And his idea of a life well-lived is to be able to supply that need.

I wonder what Senator George would have rather done with those more than three decades of years that he might have felt them better spent for the good of mankind?

It is something on which to think after the day is done.

Tired, sometimes too tired to even undress and get into bed, I sit at my window and look out into the darkness. He who can see a patch of sky at night is among the fortunate. Twice fortunate is he whose piece of heaven includes a star or stars.

It's a part of the ecstasy of country living, the chance to see the ceiling of the world after the sun has gone down. And when this dome is dotted with starlight, the good in a plain, earthly mortal stirs and speaks.

What are your thoughts when you look up at a star?

Perhaps there are some who will think alike, and again, no two people may have precisely the same ponderings. This sight in the night may incite new thoughts for each beholder.

Some time ago a story by Sir Harry Lauder, the renowned Scottish singer, appeared in the *Gold Star Mother* and revealed the meaning of a star—for one. The incident held particular significance since, at the time, the great singer was torn with grief at the loss of his only son in battle. He wrote:

"A man came to my dressing room in a New York theater and told of an experience that had recently befallen him.

"Just then, in American towns, any household that had given a son to the war was entitled to place a star on the window pane. A few nights before he came ‘to see me, this man was walking down a street in New York accompanied by his wee boy.

"The boy became very interested in the lighted windows of

the houses, and clapped his hands when he saw a star. As they passed house after house he would say, 'Oh, look, Daddy, there's another house that has given a son! And there's another! There's one with two stars! And look! There's a house with no star at all!'

"At last they came to a break in the houses. Through the gap could be seen the evening star shining brightly in the sky. The little fellow caught his breath:

" 'Oh look, Daddy,' he cried, 'God must have given His Son, for He has got a star in His window.' "

Always, a glimpse of the sky and a star has sent the spirit soaring. In their presence, grossness slips away like a cloud of mist and the better part of one's intangible self takes on form, strength, and stature. At such times, a star may be a symbol.

Henry E. Kershner, writing in the publication *Christian Economics*, delivered something of a poetic oration entitled: "On Being a Star." He wrote:

". . . I think of the lines of the old song:

> 'Hold your lighted lamp on high,
> Be a star in someone's sky.'

"Many people have lost their sense of direction and in a dark night of discouragement and confusion are looking for a star. Have you ever been a star in someone's sky?

". . . All of us can develop sufficient character, integrity and general worthiness to make us, occasionally at least, appear as stars to some who are striving to find their way in the dark."

It would seem that all that is seen is individually interpreted by those who see. Lord Albemarle once came upon his lady looking up longingly at a star. Said the lord: "Don't look at it that way, my dear—I can't buy it for you."

An all-important need for every human being is something to which to look forward. It isn't enough to have had a wonderful past. Indeed, when sorrow wrings the last drop of joy from your heart, looking back on happy years can be anguish of the worst kind.

Well-meaning people will say: "But be thankful for the happiness that you have had." And then, sometimes when the circumstances warrant such philosophy, they will add: "'Better to have loved and lost than never to have loved at all.'"

They forget that living is not so static.

We cannot exist on what has previously transpired—the spirit, like the body, must have current nourishment. Remembering last week's steak dinner is not going to fill your stomach tonight.

Quick in the course of recalling other days and other pleasant happenings comes that awful decree: "But it's gone—all gone. I'm alone now—with nothing, with no one!"

Then it is that we must make it our business to resurrect a long-time yearning, or hope, or ambition—and go to work on it. We must stoke the coals of some desire and thus lighten our darkness.

It may be as simple as acquiring a stray kitten.

Just what it is doesn't really matter at all, as long as it holds for you a clear, pure joy—as long as it remains a bright spark on your mental horizon that glows, regardless of problems and uncertainties, fears and misgivings. It is a sorry person who hasn't a star to turn to when there is nothing save gray gloom everywhere else.

Trials come to us all.

Fathers lose their jobs; mothers' automatic washers break down; friends disappoint us; and children go astray. But if we can for a moment turn our gaze to something that is a light in our lives, the somber side of life seems less somber, and the load loses some of its weight.

No doubt most everyone, if he will brush away his frustrations and self-pity and discouragements, will find a star, a star that only needs to be polished up a bit.

No doubt the man who drives the big highway mower past our house, cutting the grass and weeds along the berm of the road; or the fellow who carries in the soft water cylinder twice each month, toting his unwieldy load to the basement; or the scavenger who picks up our tin cans—all have a pot of happiness at the end of their rainbows that keeps them going when the going gets tough.

It is not a matter of money always, or even a thing of magnitude that makes us glad. More often than not, these little shining interests have no price tag, and may be wholly without worth to anyone save ourselves.

I am thinking of the granny afghan I made here a while back. With every day busy with innumerable responsibilities and necessary chores, there seemed little time for any extra activity. So, eager to crowd in this extra piece of handiwork, I set aside one hour—no more, no less—after supper in which to crochet the small woolen squares for the afghan.

A dozen times each day, I found myself looking forward to that hour after supper.

Many times, the object of our enthusiasm isn't within easy reach. And that, too, has its advantages. It steps up our anticipation.

A good book may have to be read in snatches—a line or two as we ride a bus on our way to work. Or maybe while we are waiting for the rolls to rise. Just recently a woman told of her life-time longing for a college education. It was the gleaming hope off yonder. But the fact that she had to wait didn't dim her avid ambition. No, it was for years the one ray of light in her dreary stretch of drudgery. It was something to turn to or dream about. And finally, when she was sixty years old, she launched forth into a higher education. She enrolled in a local college, graduating at sixty-four . . . having followed her star and reached her goal.

Sometimes our fondest hope is never realized. Way off in the distance it sparkles, and we travel and travel all the way through life and never reach it. Couples spend their lives drawing and altering and making additions to a dream house that never gets built. They plan for a child that is never born, for a business advancement that never comes. But that doesn't change the precious value of having something to climb toward. It has made the path easier keeping an eye on a goal. It has been a candle ever burning that has made the dark places less dark.

Better to have had a star that never came into fulfillment than never to have had a star at all . . . to better paraphrase that old, oft-quoted adage.

10.

Seek And Ye Shall Find

Rarely can one sit on the fence and watch the crops grow. But well you might if the crop happens to be dandelions, or ragweed, or thistle. Make no mistake, if it's anything of any value, you have to hop down, grab a hoe, and heave to.

This same country philosophy is applicable to every field of endeavor. Wishing will not make it happen. And that is true, whether one is doggedly determined to become a sky diver, lose thirty pounds, or find a suitable tenant for the back bedroom—the last having no connection with the noble desire to find a suitable partner with whom to march to the altar. Not that it cannot happen. No one is going to be so naive as to think that a lone, unattached male can be in the house with a lone, unattached female and not run the risk of a developing affection. However, only "gutter mammas" are going to resort to such crude methods to latch onto romance. And so, for that very reason, a lone, unattached female is going to weigh the matter of taking any member of the opposite sex into her domicile. There is the matter of propriety, too. That is, unless she has a woman companion who makes her home with her; or, the landlady herself is no less than ninety-two, wears her skirts to her ankles, her hair in a bun, and sits by the hour cross-stitching "I HATE MEN" on sofa throws, pillow tops, and possibly tea towels. And even that could prove a challenge.

That debate of the ages: "Is it easier to rent rooms to men or to women?" has never been definitely settled. And probably never will. That is because it is, in the main, a matter of individual preference. There are women who would argue until doomsday that they would never rent a room to a woman—that women are forever washing out things, which means they are always pressing something. True. They also run up water bills by taking a bath in the morning and one again when they get home from work. It's hard to believe anyone could be that dirty. Then too, many of them wash their hair so often you wonder it doesn't come loose from the scalp and fall out. All this, besides stepping up the usage of electricity by way of a hair dryer.

There are other pitfalls, too. A woman, if she is fair to look upon and pleasant to have about, is likely to appear thusly to the masculine segment of the world. Which means she may have gentlemen callers. And if she does, how are you going to know the character and caliber of the men who may come?

Renting to a man is better in this respect. If they are going to keep company with ladies, they will by necessity have to go out to carry on their social life. But any little mother-hen-of-a-landlady can't keep from lying awake and worrying when some sweet young man living in her home has not shown up by dawn.

But, on the other hand, any well-brought-up lad with a willingness to help can be real handy in opening a stubborn can, burning the trash, and even contributing the very wonderful service of taking a dead mouse out of a trap.

Besides all this, any gracious gentleman tenant one might choose is not going to let his lady landlord shovel off any snow in the winter. Make no mistake: A man in the house can be advantageous. There are also disadvantages. For instance, it is a plain nuisance to have to forever take care that you are adequately and properly clothed. There is no hopping out of bed in your nightgown and running out to the kitchen in your bare feet to get a glass of milk. Ah, no. One must get dressed. And not look like a siren in a red-light district, either, even in her own home, if there is a man rooming there.

Sometimes, this can be most annoying.

And what about smoking? And what about drinking? And what about using the telephone? You know, even the most affable roomer, male or female, can make a telephone call to the other end of the continent and move out the next day, leaving you to pay the bill.

There is the matter of the kitchen, too. Are you going to allow your paying guests to make use of the stove and refrigerator? And what about their carrying food to their rooms to eat? In carpeted bedrooms, this can be a problem. Or do you have a sure-fire way of removing coffee stains? And maybe the awful mark from a spoonful of apple butter that missed the toast?

These are important issues to set straight before you lay a key in the hand of that strange somebody, and the suitcases and boxes start making a trail through the house.

We once heard of a woman who typed off a list of rules for prospective renters. It included things like: "Don't walk across the bedroom without shoes. There is a board that squeaks only when it's trod upon by bare feet," "Any radio or television must be turned off not later than 10 P.M." And, "The toilet must be flushed no more than twice in 24 hours."

With such a stipulation as the last, it is presumed the landlord made proper allowance on the rent for purchases of spray deodorants or room fresheners.

Our source of information, who happened to need a room, took one look at the list of rules and went back to his car to check the classified ads for another room.

Locating someone both responsible and congenial to share your hearth and home may be simmered down to the Biblical admonition: "Seek and ye shall find." And if you seek long enough, you are bound to find someone who suits you. Sometimes leaving one's name and address at a nearby school will land a teacher. Sometimes a suitable roomer may be found through simply passing the word around at the places you shop. And then again, there is always the newspaper.

An advertisement need not be long, just clearly stated as to location, nature of accommodations, and, of course, the sort of tenant you most desire. That's important. If you are dead set against renting to women, well, make it plain. Your ad might read:

> Southside suburban, first floor, room with private bath. Business man only. Phone: 0-0000.

If you would really like a lady, but want her as little under foot as possible, well, indicate that fact. As a suggestion:

> On Garfield Park bus line: Big upstairs room with adjoining sleeping porch. Kitchen privileges. For employed lady. Phone: 0-0000.

Save the exact address for later divulgence. And do not be too quick to divulge. After all, you don't want to land on a filing card of Robert the Raper. When people call, talk to them awhile. Ask them about themselves. Tell them that you like to know something about the folks who come to live at your house. After all, it's important that people who are coming to live under the same roof have some knowledge of one another, their habits and way of life.

With just a little conversation, one can detect the character of the caller. For instance, if he gives his place of employment, and perhaps even mentions a social or fraternal connection. So it is, one can try to size up an applicant.

Any honest, understanding soul will accept all this and patiently describe his situation and precise need. If he gets agitated, even indignant—very well. This is the time to root him out. And keep your address to yourself.

Vitally necessary is the marital status.

If it develops that a couple has had a spat the night before, and the husband is gathering up his belongings and getting himself a room and moving—bow out. Let him go to the Y.M.C.A. and cool off. The same goes for a hot-headed wife. Only you had better recommend the Y.W.C.A.

There's no point in getting in the middle of a fight, or supplying assistance in separating a couple. Anyway, before the sun goes down again, they may have made up and you will have lost a tenant.

Introducing any disturbed, discordant, or unstable situation into one's home is sheer folly—there are too many wonderful, happily poised people about in need of the room you have to offer. By elimination, they can be found.

Neatness and personal appearance can be taken into account with the first interview. Do not think that anyone who comes to look at a room who is slovenly put together and not too clean is going to change when he or she moves into your home. Don't be so stupid! Checking on the renting of a room is a piece of business. And anyone on such a mission should be appropriately clad.

And that does not mean women coming in slacks or shorts.

117

Not that wearing such attire is a road to Hades, but being thusly dressed on such an occasion is in poor taste. And would indicate a type of thinking that is careless. And bear in mind, you are looking for someone careful, dependable, and a credit to your home.

Of course, quite soon in the interchange of information, the smart landlord will ask for references. There should be no fewer than three. With someone who is presently active in business, it would quite naturally be a representative of that firm, a bank or store at which the applicant has been a patron, and a church reference. For the one who is about to take a stranger into his home, no stone should be left unturned in ascertaining the character of the individual who is to have access to your property. And, although you yourself may be no churchgoer, it is a fact that people with some religious affiliation are better risks. They are more likely to have a standard of conduct that will cause them to be respectful of you and your home, and so behave themselves becomingly. It is always comforting to have a good word from an applicant's minister, or rabbi, or priest. Or, perhaps, simply a fellow member of the respective denomination.

It is even better if your prospective roomer is really active in his or her church. Maybe a member of the Men's Bible Class or the Cheerful Doers Women's Circle. A mere name on a mere roster says little. For the woman alone who is trying to make use of her empty house in filling her empty life, the added money from a room rented is not the only consideration.

You want no scalawags; nobody mean and despicable who might tuck an oriental rug under his arm and walk off, bring bedbugs into the house, or come home loaded. This person you are about to take into your home must be first-rate, someone who not only looks respectable but can offer proof of a good present as well as an honorable past.

They can be found—that is, if you continue to seek.

Whether they are to be young or very young, old or very old, or simply a nice, comfortable and reliable middle-age is worthy of consideration. There is something to be said in favor of every generation. Each period of life has its tendencies. The challenge is in being able to adjust to that which generally goes along with the inclinations of the age levels. You cannot put an old head on young shoulders. So if you rent a room to a twenty-year-old youngster, well, then be prepared to have the icebox stuffed full of soft drinks, and a record player going half the night. And you may not have much chance to use your own telephone.

All this goes along with youth. But if your spirits have been dragging bottom lately, if you're lonely and feeling as though you were a thousand years old—a little youngness could be just what you need. Such an experience can remind you of the time when your own kids were home and the house was bursting with life.

So it was with older folks, those who have gotten tottery and forgetful, and maybe even crochety—they can bring to mind your mamma or your dad, or your old Uncle George. And it can be a sweet joy to help these dear ones feel loved; to take time to visit with them, and do what you can to make their days happy.

Doing for others is still the best way to find a purpose for being about. And taking someone into your home offers many opportunities for being kind to the wanderer who has found shelter in your harbor.

It never ceases to be amazing how much people need people. The very fact that someone has come to you to rent a room is indicative of the fact that he is, at least momentarily, disjointed from his usual habitat . . . certainly, uprooted from former moorings, perhaps near family and friends. And so for that very reason, he needs the kindly thoughtfulness and little generosities that a really gracious homemaker is in a position to confer.

Surprises are always welcome. It is rather nice to come home and find a just-plucked rose from the garden in a bud vase by one's bedside. Or possibly, a book from your own library that would seem to be in line with your roomer's particular tastes and interests. Or what about an invitation to Sunday morning breakfast?

There are endless ways by which to encompass a paying guest with a feeling of home and hospitality. Put yourself in his position, and it will come easy, the instinct of knowing what to do and when to do it.

And here's the magic of it all: In the expending of thought and energy in behalf of the other person or persons sharing one's domicile, the woman alone loses that wretched feeling of being alone. Not only is there company in the house—always a safety measure—but there is someone about who needs kindness. And in the giving, she who has in some manner been bereft and left on her own finds purpose. The crushed spirit takes a deep breath and revives when it finds an avenue of usefulness. It could be in getting out and getting a job. That is a goodly solution if one is young enough and able. And then it could be in utilizing the facilities of one's home, in providing a comfortable place of lodging where happiness waits for those who need just that.

And where is the human being who does not need the warmth and cheer of other human beings, whether it is in coming home to a rented room, or in the chap who sacks up the oranges at the fruit market?

Katie Comstock is not really alone, in the sense of being bereaved and a widow. Not at all. Her Boyd, her husband of well-nigh thirty years, is hale and healthy, but so involved in his job as a salesman that he is gone most of the time. Apparently he works three times as hard as he did during his younger days, and makes half as much. All this makes for a pinched budget. Not young herself anymore, Katie found herself with too much time alone, too many hours in which to worry and fret.

One night, as she sat at the dinette window looking out into the darkness, waiting for Boyd to come home from seeing a prospect, she picked up the evening paper. As she leafed through, her eye fell on extra black letters heading a classified advertisement. It read: "ROOMS WANTED."

A stock company setting up plays for summer theatricals needed rooms for their directors, producers, and visiting actors and actresses. The advertisement specified that rooms were needed in the locality of the big theater-in-the-round tent. That happened to be in Katie's part of town.

She talked to Boyd when he got home shortly after one o'clock in the morning. It was all right with him. Katie answered the ad the following morning.

That was three summers ago. Since then, Katie's life has been one long line of theatrical people and the accompanying excitement that goes with meeting folk she had seen in the movies and on television. Thankful for a pleasant place to stay and Katie's motherly attentions, the show people have showered their sweet landlady with affection: tickets to the shows, little gifts for the house and for Katie, but best of all talk times.

Faye Emerson, in town for a play, stopped around to see the director, who has stayed at Katie's for several summers. It was early in the morning and the director was not ready.

Katie said to Faye: "Come on around to the side yard, and let's sit under the pear tree and have a cup of coffee."

Faye was delighted, so she and her two dogs, which were in the car with her, joined Katie in lawn chairs scattered about in the shade. And for almost twenty minutes they sat and chatted

and sipped coffee. Yes, and enjoyed some of Katie's snickerdoo-
dles. That's a cookie she makes that all the show people love.

Throughout the year, Katie's mail is fun. The various perform-
ers who have stayed at her home during the run of a play often
write back when they go on the road again.

Some of them have continued the correspondence. Some of
them telephone occasionally—at Christmas, on Mother's Day.
When playing at nearby towns, they have sent tickets and written to ask Katie to come and bring Boyd.

So it is these members of the entertainment world have expressed their appreciation for the homelike atmosphere and
motherly attention they experienced while staying at Katie's
house. They have not forgotten the times when the light was left
burning on the patio when they arrived, and Katie was sitting up
waiting with a pitcher of ice-cold lemonade. And always with an
eagerness to hear how the show had gone that night. After the
tense hours of speaking lines, they loved the chance to unwind
and relax. And talk. And to have someone to listen.

Perhaps if none of us had any more to give to the world than a
listening ear, we would find a warm, affectionate place in the
hearts of everyone within our radius. Men and women, whatever
their social stratum and field of interest, always welcome someone to listen.

For years now, Katie has listened to the folks who have rented
her rooms. And in return, her knowledge of the theater has
grown; she has widened her circle of friends, and found contentment in an inner esteem from supplying an essential need in
the lives of others. And doing it in plus fashion—adding a host of
little extras. Maybe a cake and candles for some of her people
having birthdays. Maybe a knitted stole or socks as a going-away
present—a bit of handiwork turned out on Katie's own needles.

Of course, the money collected as room rent cannot be belittled. The added income from Katie's venture has done its part in easing the financial squeeze. More especially, in providing a few extras that would have been impossible otherwise. For instance, Katie was able to get the living room carpeted from the income from her rooms. She has bought a new electric range. And just recently, she was able to help Boyd out on a car payment that was lagging.

How much does one charge for a room?

Only inquiry in your particular vicinity can answer that question. Much depends on how much you have to offer. Do you have a private entrance for the use of your roomer? Do you allow kitchen privileges? Or do your people simply rent a room and go out for all meals? And what about a garage for your roomer's car?

These are all matters to take into account in arriving at a just rental. However, bear in mind that you are operating no cut-rate, cheap joint. Your intentions are to give the best, so plan on charging for superior accommodations.

The high type persons whom you plan to attract to your home will be willing to pay accordingly. And will consider themselves fortunate in having such a pleasant place.

The tax help that can be realized in turning one's home into income property is worthy of consideration. Once you have received income from any portion of your house, you are automatically entitled to certain deductions tax-wise.

Instead of having just a home, you have a business.

Whatever fraction of your property is being rented, that same fraction can be applied in your deductions on real estate tax, insurance, maintenance, laundry of linens, dry cleaning of curtains, utilities, household help, etc. For instance, if you have a six-room house and rent out two rooms, two-sixths of the expenses on your house are deductible on your Federal Income Tax Report.

Such savings contribute their part in this all-over plan to enrich and make happy the days of a woman left alone with a house and a sad heart. Sorrow feels its first healing touch when she who grieves finds some service she can render others.

It can be inside her own four walls.

Just now, however, it was time to set the table. Uncle Cliff and Aunt Doris were coming for supper. As always, company put a glow on the moment.

11.

The Therapy Of Boys And Girls

It is important, now and then, to be made to feel one is really quite amazing and wonderful.

In fact, there is a little something inside us all that withers up and shrinks into oblivion, unless occasionally it gets a generous feeding of unadulterated adoration. One very pleasant form comes in the way of wet, sticky kisses that may leave behind a smudge of raspberry jam. And perchance, little chubby arms that knock glasses to the ground, play havoc with your hair-do, but wrap your very soul in the ecstasy of being loved.

Humankind's hunger for affection never ends. It's as real and eager at ninety as it was at nine. Put your arm around some elderly relative, some friend or neighbor; plant a kiss on his cheek and watch the joy and the glow that comes into his face. It is shameful how stingy most of us are with our affection. A little pat, a little hug, a word of tenderness can help sick people get well, lone people to feel less alone.

In the attempt to reorganize and rebuild a way of life, the lone one, man or woman, will find that time and attention given to children within their sphere can put an important ingredient into existence.

Youngsters make good friends.

And in dropping our grown-up cloak to companion with a child, one also drops some of the grown-up heaviness of spirit. By a little imagination and effort, a vast array of chummy activities can bridge the gap between the adult and the tot next door, or the family of kids across the street. Or still better, your own children or grandchildren, your nieces and nephews. Maybe even some small cousins that you had never noticed much before.

Too much verbiage has been devoted to what interested adults can contribute to the lives of children. It is time we give a thought to what little people can do for big people.

Children are well equipped with some of the noble, wholesome virtues that their elders have somehow lost along the way. Besides their readiness to heap love and esteem on any oldster who might grant them the very privilege of putting raisin buttons down the fat tummy of a gingerbread man, theirs is the knack of forgiveness.

Little ones are incapable of hanging on to a grudge, or distrust, or an old hate.

Seeing their innocence about many things is like catching a glimpse of clear blue sky in between seething banks of menacing clouds. Even television has not wholly obliterated this clean, good quality—at least from the very young. Nor has it totally obsessed those of few years with an attitude of sophistication.

To behold the open-eyed wonder of children is gently renewing. That's why there is recuperation for any sad and lonely person.

With the consent and cooperation of a child's parents, plan some little venture that youngsters might enjoy. In the experience, the grown-up sponsor enjoys something of the child's eagerness and excitement. Dozens of birthdays are whittled away as an adult trots alongside some little person. Indeed, there comes an urge to skip instead of walk, and whistle as you go.

Bruce was seven years old when the two of us took off for St. Louis and the Mississippi River. On the Christmas before, he had gotten a copy of a child's book on Samuel Clemens, who grew up and became America's famous Mark Twain. We had talked about it, how St. Louis was in the vicinity of Hannibal, Missouri, where the creator of Huckleberry Finn and Tom Sawyer had lived. As a boy, Samuel Clemens had sauntered along the river's edge and dreamed dreams.

Once, when the family had gone into town and Bruce had to stay home and nurse a bad cold, the two of us talked about the Mississippi River. By the time the folks had returned, the small boy had learned how to spell the name of the Father of Waters, as Mamma had taught me. Said the lad to his parents:

"Listen, you say it like this: M-i-double-s, i-double-s, i-double-p, i."

And then we announced our plans for the coming summer. Bruce and his auntie were going to St. Louis and take a trip on the M-i-double-s, i-double-s, i-double-p, i. That is, with approval from headquarters.

Syd and Louise went along with the idea.

Some few months later, the whole clan went to the airport to see us off. Young Bruce had just learned to tell time, so he kept watching the big clock in the air depot and telling us how many minutes until flight time.

And then, from out of the sky swooped the silver monster. It was the plane for St. Louis.

Aboard, the little blond boy in a bow tie and long pants snuggled up beside his aunt: "I just can't believe it, Mimi," he said. "I just can't."

People were settling themselves into the maroon-colored seats.

Some were already reading newspapers. One woman was hard at work on a crossword puzzle. Two young service men were leaning back, preparing to take a nap. Such indifference. No one seemed thrilled. It was easy to feel sorry for people without zest, people who failed to get a rise out of the prospect of rising above the earth—for everybody who did not have a little boy to take to see the Mississippi River.

Then—then it happened. There was a terrific roar. The landing wheels slipped gently up, and we left the earth. Higher. Higher. Higher. After a while, the hostess spoke into a public address system: "You are flying at 8,000 feet and at 210 miles per hour."

The earth looked neat and well ordered. There were great squares in varying shades of green, with tiny ribbons of road running between.

Suddenly, we plunged into a mass of seething white. It was a cloud world. It was a beautiful world that changed from moment to moment. It looked like a countryside covered with snow. Then again, it looked as if we were riding over mounds of feathers. The earth was no longer visible. There was white below and white above.

The hostess came up the aisle and laid her hand on Bruce's shoulder. "Would you like to go up and have a visit with the pilots?"

The boy at my side was on his feet instantly. Saying not a word, he hurried down the aisle beside the gracious young hostess. Seconds later, I discovered that the pilots had put a set of earphones on the little guy.

We first saw the Mississippi River from the air—a darkish strip, separating the East from the West. Later we saw it from the banks of the river itself.

We talked about the different names the Mississippi had had

in the course of time. Cortez, the conqueror of Mexico, made a map in 1520. He called the river "Rio-del-Spiritu Sancto" (River of the Holy Ghost). Others called it Chucaquax Palisado, Escondido. But it was the Indian name "Mech-ese-be," meaning Great Waters, which stuck. Marquette used this Indian name, as we do today, only we spell it a little differently.

Home seemed far away as young Bruce and his auntie looked out upon the river from the bank of the Mississippi. In the company of the child, the gloom of recent sorrow seemed to break up and scatter like rain clouds on a spring day. It is impossible to feel heavy and mentally weighed down when there is an excited youngster at your side.

So gently the excited, youthful outlook moves in and replaces the gray depression. The wonder with which young minds behold that which their eyes chance to see is catching. One finds oneself falling into the gleeful gladness of the small girl or boy. Comes exuberance.

There were boats of varying sizes out on the river and anchored at shore. Tied up at the wharf and loading passengers was the beautiful S.S. *Admiral.*

Once on board we obtained a pamphlet describing the luxurious ship. Bruce pulled a deck chair over to the railing of the top deck and sat down. I took a place beside him. For a while we were both silent. There was so much to see. For one thing, the wide stretch of muddy water that was all around. It lapped against the sides of the boat, but the great silver hull stood unmovable and still.

I opened the pamphlet and began to read aloud. And the little boy in the deck chair listened. Said the descriptive folder:

"The S. S. *Admiral* is the largest river passenger steamer ever built in America. It is over one block long. It carries 5,000 passengers, and has a crew of more than 200, and two orchestras. There are five decks and two elevators. . . ."

We left the wharf at 10 A.M. and started downstream at 12 knots per hour. Oh, yes, we got quite nautical before the six-hour journey was over. We learned several other seagoing terms—even met the captain, Verne Streckfus, one of the owners of the Streckfus Line. We learned that many years ago the elder Streckfus started the steamship concern. And then his four sons continued the operation of the line.

It was a happy crowd aboard the *Admiral*. There were, perhaps, 500 children playing on deck "A." Slowly, gracefully, the laughing, light-hearted cargo made its way down the Mississippi. There was lunch on the *Admiral* at noon, and then it turned and started back to St. Louis.

Adults of all ages raced around the ship checking up on all the missing kids. There were many young parents. And there were others that looked like grandmothers and grandfathers. Occasionally, there was a lone man or a lone woman walking along the deck with a child clasping his hand.

Perhaps he too was seeking escape in the company of young buoyancy.

Attaching oneself to a child or, for that matter, to many children requires no long-drawn-out procedure. If nature has, through natural processes, bestowed on you your own little sons and daughters, grandsons and granddaughters, nieces, nephews, or small cousins, the opportunity to cultivate youthful companionship is ready-made. However, if succeeding generations have not turned up in your clan—there are always the neighbors and their offspring.

Helen and Luke Hausier had only the one child, twelve-year-old Casey. They were a fun-loving little trio. That is, when they could all be together. Helen worked as a file clerk for an engineering firm and Luke sold air conditioners.

It was on an August afternoon, shortly after Helen had returned from lunch, that the bell rang on her extension phone. It was the hospital calling. Casey, riding his bicycle, had been hit by a car. She must come at once.

Helen phoned Luke's office. He was out. She left word, then leaped from her desk and started down the hall weeping. One of the senior draftsmen passed her enroute to the elevator and drove her to the hospital.

They were there in minutes. But not soon enough. Casey was dead. So ended a chapter in Helen and Luke Hausier's life. They were parents no longer. There was no child to plan for, to save for, to take on weekend camping trips in the woods.

Helen was practically out of her mind with grief. Because she would burst into tears suddenly and uncontrollably, and then tremble for hours thereafter, her physician insisted that she give up her job and stay home for a long rest.

With more time on her hands, she lapsed into dark, sullen periods followed by the violent weeping. Helen's sister, Mabel, tried to talk to her:

"Your boy's father is sad, too. Don't forget that. You are not making it any easier on him. You're giving Luke no comfort at all."

The summer passed. And on a Saturday afternoon in mid-October, Luke coaxed Helen to come outside and help him rake leaves. That's what they were doing when three-year-old Theresa came running up the front walk. She and her mother, who lived two doors down the block, were on their way to the corner to drop a letter in the mailbox. Fascinated by the mountain of leaves in the Hausier's front yard, Theresa had broken away and come nearer to see the golden heap.

That's how it happened. That's how Helen and Luke and Theresa became acquainted. It so happened that the little girl's mamma was expecting another baby momentarily. There was a need for someone with whom to leave Theresa for a few weeks.

So began a new era in the lives of the bereaved parents. Helen pulled her old portable sewing machine out of the back closet and made herself and Theresa matching aprons. And then after that came doll clothes. One evening on his way home from work, Luke stopped by the lumber yard and picked up lumber to build a playhouse in the backyard.

"Really, it's a good idea," said Luke. "If Theresa should move away, we could convert it into a tool house."

But Theresa and her family did not move away. Instead, over a period of years, there was one baby after another. And each time, Theresa and the other little ones would come to Aunt Helen and Uncle Luke's sometime during their mother's absence.

Helen had gone back to her old job a few months after meeting little Theresa. Once on a Saturday afternoon in early December when she was bringing four of the children home after taking them downtown to see Santa Claus, Helen said to their mother:

"Let me know ahead if ever there is going to be another baby, so I can arrange to have my vacation at that time."

Said the young mother: "Well, plan on the last of June. And you might as well know. If it's a girl, it's going to be Helen. And if it's a boy, it's going to be Luke. I couldn't have had these kids without the help of you folks."

Helen was silent for a time, and then she said: "Theresa kept me from going insane. These children have put something into our lives that Luke and I desperately needed. It's been wonderful to have youngsters to love and to love us ... wonderful!"

The Russells, who live in one of the town's more exclusive suburban subdivisions, never had any children. And they did not especially miss them. However, by the time they were in their late seventies, their world, as Carl Russell aptly expressed it, became more and more bounded by the front porch and the back gate.

They did not feel up to running off to Florida in the winter and Minnesota in the summer. And so they stayed home. But even so, they saw less and less of their old friends and neighbors.

Carl's wife said: "We have become survivors of a dead past, two lonely waifs lost in a sea of busy people."

"Heck, honey," said Carl, "you're getting mighty poetic about the situation. It's not that beautiful being a couple of old rusty boxcars pulled in on a siding."

"Now, listen here," said Maude Russell, "I refuse to be likened to a boxcar. And I certainly don't appreciate the idea of becoming rusty. You stay home and mind the tree trimmers this afternoon, and I'm going downtown to shop for a new dress."

Shortly after the top off a big Chinese elm had come down, Carl was stalking around, poking his cane into the bramble of boughs.

"Hey!" he called to one of the tree men. "Mind coming here with your saw? Mind cutting away the branches and getting me that fork? It's just right for a sling shot!"

That afternoon, Carl sat in the sun on a garden bench in the side yard and skinned the bark from the fork, whittled it into shape, and then combed the garage looking for an old inner tube.

"You gotta have rubber," he explained to Maude.

So began Carl's sling shot hobby, which captured the fancy of nine-year-old Tommy next door, and later eleven-year-old Jim in the next block, and still later ten-year-old William across the street. Some time afterward, when another Chinese elm had to be topped, Carl had the boys all come over and hunt forks. And then he gave them a lesson in making really elegant sling shots. Right along with all of this came definite instructions on how to use a sling shot, and how not to use it. Older people in the neighborhood heard of Carl's new project and stopped around to take a look at what their retired friend was doing. Before they left, they usually wound up by placing an order for a sling shot for their young grandson or nephew—or a joker gift for some man of their acquaintance.

So it was that new friendships developed. The kids who got sling shots knew other kids who wanted sling shots; and all of these youngsters had parents whom Maude and Carl enjoyed meeting. In fact, when the forks ran low, several families planned a trip to the country, with Carl heading the pack on a fork-hunting expedition.

Hear this label which was attached to one sling shot that found its way to our house:

GENUINE WALRUS WALLOPER AND CAMEL CONKER

Now, after five or six years, Carl is still at it. Yes, now deep in his eighties. Says Maude: "To be less lonely in that sea of busy people is to do something to attract at least part of the sea to your door."

Adds Carl: "That's right. Even if it's only a wave or two."

Awakening to what one has missed in not taking unto oneself a spouse and having children can come late. It can come after the elderly mother with whom one has lived and whom one has worked and supported has passed to other shores. It can come after one has retired from a job that has filled one's life for forty years or more. No one feels more left out than that person who sees his contemporaries going places and doing things with children and grandchildren, nieces and nephews, while he himself is pigeonholed with a few adult loners. It's the moment of reckoning for those who somehow never got around to establishing a home and family. Or, to put it more bluntly, to getting married and having a baby.

Dorothy White was one of those people. It was just a year or two after her mother's death and her own retirement as a legal secretary that the oppression of her aloneness began to bear down upon her. Her usual buoyant spirits began to sag once she was out of her eight-to-five routine and the demands of home and an aging parent.

In appraising her situation, it appeared that in her retirement she had become simply a name on the roster of a half-dozen or more clubs. And yet it was her association with one of those groups that opened new fields of activity. First, it welded a warm, comfortable tie between her and a little child. And then later, hundreds of children.

That organization was the National Audubon Society. When a young mother living near Dorothy's home asked Dorothy if she could care for her four-year-old Kim so the mother could take a job, Dorothy said:

"Yes, if I can take him with me as I take a spring census of the birds." The enumeration necessitated daily walks, over a period of a few weeks, within a ten-block radius of Dorothy's home.

Said the mother: "Kim would like that. And it would be good for him to be out of doors."

Shortly after the boy's arrival each morning, Dorothy would button him up in his sweater and take him by the hand, and together they would start forth on foot.

"'ook!" young Kim would cry, "D'ere is a robin."

"Now, Kim," Dorothy would reply, "you know better than

that. That is a jay." And then the retired secretary would stop and explain to the little boy that a robin had an orange-red breast and the jay was bright blue. Back home again, they would get out the drawing paper and crayons and Kim would draw a robin and a jay and color them.

As Dorothy tucked the child into bed for his afternoon nap, she would tell him stories having to do with birds. She might tell him about the woodpecker, who was a carpenter and could hammer away on a tree. Or again, it might be about the chickadee, who had a habit of calling out his name so brightly and cheerfully: "Chicka-dee-dee, chicka-dee-dee."

Some time later, the local Audubon Society needed someone to meet Audubon lecturers coming into the community to speak and show nature films. One of the duties was to accompany the lecturers to various public schools in the area where they could present a program.

Dorothy offered to take the position. After all, she had had the experience of talking to little Kim. Why couldn't she stand up before a roomful of boys and girls, make a few remarks about wildlife, and introduce a National Audubon Society speaker who would tell them a great deal more about birds?

This project and the details involved have vastly widened Dorothy's scope. It has not only made it possible for her to become closely acquainted with well-known Audubon Society lecturers, but it has brought her into contact with numerous teachers, some of whom have become intimate friends. More important, it has brought flocks of children into her life. In fact, they call her on the phone and ask for help in identifying unknown birds. Or write her letters for information. Not infrequently, a dozen or more youngsters will troop along beside Dorothy on a Saturday afternoon bird hike.

Even though he has gotten to be twelve years old and does

not really need a "sitter" anymore, Kim is always along. Indeed, nobody would be surprised if Kim turned out to be a National Audubon Society lecturer. He has become that much of an authority on birds. And it looks as though he might have a future in such a field. Says Dorothy:

"Teaching children about the outdoors is one way of counteracting juvenile delinquency. It's also a way of crowding a spinster's life so full of youthful associations that she hasn't got time to get old, or lonesome."

Lilly Holmes had known the full meaning of being a wife and a mother, and a grandmother. Only now she was a widow; and the children were married, living far away in homes of their own.

The emptiness and the quietness of the house were slowly making Lilly desperate: "I crave noise," she told a neighbor one morning, "the noise that was all around me when the kids were little."

"You want noise?" said her neighbor. "Well, how about taking care of Jodey and Jane tomorrow afternoon?"

The three-year-old twins had not been on Lilly's patio ten minutes until Lilly was not so sure about her need for clamor and confusion. It was when the girls climbed upon the patio table, preparing to jump off, that Lilly suggested that they all go into the house for a story.

She got down a copy of Grimm's *Fairy Tales,* an old, worn volume from which she had once read to her children. That's what she was doing when Jodey and Jane's mother returned. The girls did not want to go home. Lilly said, laying the book aside: "Maybe your mamma will let you come over next week, and we will read some more." She had realized by now that it wasn't the noise of the children that she craved, but the presence of children.

And that's the way it started, Aunt Lilly's Storytime. The word got around, and a couple of mothers called to ask if they could pay and have their little ones come too. If Aunt Lilly would take the tots, their mothers would be free for the afternoon.

By the time there were a dozen requests, Lilly agreed to put a nominal fee on her storytime, with a promise of milk and home-made cookies, and pallets on the floor for the kiddies who took a nap.

Now the project has overflowed into more than one afternoon, and Lilly says: "The emptiness is gone."

12.

Genial Acceptance

There are bones and there are bones. Little ones and long ones, bones of all sorts and for all reasons, but the most important bone any two-legged creature can count among his anatomical assets is his funny bone.

It was midnight, and Hilda and Mrs. Trimble and I had all unexpectedly converged at the refrigerator, each bent on a glass of ice water. Said Hilda:

"That hole in the sheet gets bigger every time I think of it."

"Hole?" said Mrs. Trimble. "There were two holes."

And at that, each of us, clad in our nightgowns, broke forth into fresh shrieks of merriment—probably for the nineteenth time since the company had left for home some two hours previously.

Leah and her husband, Dorris, just back from Hawaii, had offered to come out and show their colored slides in our living room. It turned into a surprise party for Clarence Bethuram and his wife, May, who were about to observe their forty-ninth wedding anniversary. Since they were all in the employ of the Indianapolis Main Post Office, more and more postal people were invited, until, when they arrived, there was hardly room for Miss

Fluff, the white collie, to find a place to sit down and scratch a flea.

It was a great, wonderful collection of people that had resulted from a simple little dissertation on rural mailboxes that had appeared in My Window column. Clarence, head of Patron Relations, had seen the column and sent it on to Washington, where it received due notice. And by this sequence of events had come any number of delightful friendships with the United States Post Office and its local representatives.

In the dining room, getting out Mamma's Haviland cups and saucers, I could hear the buzz of talk in the front room. Suddenly, Leah stepped around the corner:

"Honey, the afternoon sun is coming in your front windows so bright that the pictures are not going to show up. Could I have some sheets to hang over the windows?"

"Of course, Leah. If you don't mind getting them. Hilda needs me in the kitchen right now." I took her to the linen closet off the back hall, and then hurried on to the kitchen.

Minutes later, when Hilda and Mrs. Trimble and I returned to the living room, we were confronted with a sad sight. No doubt any family in the city on welfare would have had more decent-looking sheets. They were snagged and tattered, and one had a hole as big as a head in the middle. The second and third equally disreputable-looking pieces of bedding were just then being hung over the hole.

It was utterly horrible, humiliating—and hilarious. No need to explain, to make excuses, or even to yank them down and replace them with hemstitched pink percale sheets with little rosebuds on the hem line.

The damage was done. They had all seen our "holey" linen. And anyway, how was Leah to know which shelf we kept the rags on, and which the more respectable, freshly washed and ironed sheets and pillow cases?

If our ego had been somewhat inflated with the honor of entertaining such an array of officials from the U.S. Post Office, it was now laid limp. There was only one thing to do, and that was to take it lightly and laugh.

The meeting at the refrigerator started the whole thing over again. Strangely enough, it kept getting funnier.

I couldn't help but think of the hurts of time gone by that could have been dismissed with a chuckle. But when you are eighteen and on crutches, and on your first real date with a boy, it is quite unfunny to step on a wet leaf and fall full length at the feet of that real cool fellow.

Possibly, you could call them conditioning episodes; however, they are certainly not restricted to just the clumsy. Whatever one's circumstance or situation, one is pretty likely, some time or other, to get one's sensitivities bumped. God help the man or woman who has been put together minus that most essential ingredient to life, happiness, and well being: a funny bone.

Where the thing is, I wouldn't know. But it must be pretty safely tucked away, because it can't be broken. It can't be stepped on, or given a kick. It can't be bruised, neither can it be abused. And though they call it a bone, I'm inclined to believe that it is more of a gristle, because it is springy. It has resilience and bounce.

We can tumble from the heights; we can lose our best friend, our job, all of our hair and most of our front teeth. We can fall headlong into a mire of debt, misunderstanding and self-pity; but all of this and more to boot can't knock us out if we come to rest upon our funny bone. The ludicrousness, the joke of the situation, pulls us up and out, and before we know it we're on the right road again . . . and whistling as we travel.

Blessings on the funny bone!

Life up there in the clouds is all right. Austerity, high-flung phrases and stiff severity do have their places. But it would be stifling to stay forever in such an atmosphere. The human heart needs refreshment now and then. It needs fun.

Did you ever analyze the output of a really renowned speaker? Regardless of the dire import of the message, the good talker spikes his elixir with a dash of wit. It relaxes his audience. It rests him. With war, and slaughter, and taxes, there are plenty of reasons to be grim. But it is still more pleasant to grin. And nothing so helps the cause in that direction as the gentle secretion from that "pearl of great price"—the funny bone.

It's like oil. It relieves the tension. It loosens the cogs in the machinery of living and quiets the squeaks. No one really enjoys being stiff and precise. Will Rogers, the great humorist, knew that.

Once Will and Irvin S. Cobb were on their way to the White House to meet Calvin Coolidge. Said Cobb:

"I betcha you can't make the President laugh."

"It's a bet," said Will.

With due solemnity and in most proper White House form, Cobb was presented to President Coolidge. Will Rogers was next. As the two shook hands, Will Rogers and the President, Will cupped his hand over his ear and bent close:

"What's the name?" he asked.

President Coolidge leaned back his head and laughed . . . laughed as few people had ever had the privilege of hearing him laugh.

Will Rogers had touched the President's funny bone.

Like slipping on a leaf and taking a tumble on your first date, spending Thanksgiving day alone is something other than amusing.

But as important as levity is, a realistic view of one's role on life's scene is even more important. Married brothers and sisters, nieces and nephews, sons and daughters cannot always include some lone relative in their holiday plans.

Sometimes they want to take a jet and go to the other side of the world. Or, let's face it, sometimes they simply want to stay home and rest. They do not want to cook any big dinner, or accumulate a sinkful of dirty dishes; they want to don neither girdle nor shirt, nor their company manners.

One's nearest kin has a right to their own sweet aloneness when they prefer it. All of this should incite no tears in someone rather recently bereft, who, still unaccustomed to his or her solitary state, whimpers: "Where is everyone?"

Really, it should be no problem at all. Because, if you look, you can always find someone who is in the same predicament.

Only, of course, you must not be too choosy. If you start getting particular, you are likely to wind up as you are—alone.

Hear the mental cogs go 'round.

"Well, there's Clida Mae. I could call her and we could go out and have dinner together. Only Clida Mae always wants to hash over her perpetual feud with her boss.

"And then there is dear old Uncle Mac, who was our neighbor for so many years. His one child, Bill, is married and lives in Florida and has forgotten how to write. Uncle Mac, who lives by himself, fills his whole life with armchair politics. And just now, with things turning out as they have in the county, he would spend the whole day gloating over the GOP victory. And at the moment I'm not up to it. I'd be bound to crack off!

"'Course I could get in the mood of the occasion and cook up a nice dinner, turkey and all the trimmings, for Cousin Evelyn, who lives in a retirement home. But Evelyn doesn't like turkey and what's Thanksgiving dinner without turkey?"

Really, the business of getting through holidays solo style rates research and analysis. Maybe even a syndicated newspaper series reaching from Yucatan to Ypsilanti. Certainly there is no corner of the country without its lone souls who, by one turn of destiny or another, find themselves separated from friends and kin on some special day.

And getting married and having a lot of children is not always gilt-edge insurance. Even then, one can eventually become a leftover. After all, there is Father Time and his scythe. And kids do grow up and go away. And sometimes money is a little short for you to get to them, or for them to get to you.

Falling short of the accepted and traditional family image is upsetting. Since that first day of thanks was declared, the Thanksgiving dinner table has been envisioned as a kind of re-union spot. There is Papa at one end and Mamma at the other. Of course there is always a grandpa or a grandma, and children and more children, of all ages and sizes. Interspersed about the food-laden board is usually an aunt or two, and an uncle, and any number of cousins.

It is too bad that some smart publicity artist has not glamor-ized lone people on a holiday, perhaps eating a fried egg sand-wich at a dinette table, with no one about but the cat. Any Scrooge would be quick enough to point out certain problems that arise when a conclave of folks assemble for a meal. For instance, you can count on it that some of the crowd will be late. And, of course, that means those who got there on time are going to have to eat warmed-over biscuits.

It's a crumb of comfort for the loner to nibble on as he pads around his quarters in mid-afternoon still in his bathrobe. He may even tell himself that being alone and quiet is just what he needed. If so, he had better keep it a secret. Let it out and he will not be alone. Somebody, upon learning of his state, will whisk him off, quick as a wink, to share his hearth and victuals. Americans who love America, and people who love people, are just that way.

All of this can cause the proud loner to retreat.

It's not that we are denying a yearning for tenderness, a longing to be necessary to another's happiness, but the chance that we are being an object of pity is horrifying. And so what do we do? Out of a fear of imposing, we leap behind a defense of independence, that shaky superstructure of pride.

No, we do not want anyone to give up his usual place on the front seat of the car for us. No, we want no plans changed, altered, or even made especially for our convenience. No, we would ask no favors, expect no special consideration, nor accept any out-of-the-ordinary bestowals of time, money handouts, or attention. If anyone has to sleep on the cot in the dining room, it will be the cat. No one is going to sacrifice his good bed for our comfort. We'll go home.

The whole problem is an inability to graciously receive, or take and take it nicely. It's high time somebody said something about accepting thoughtful gestures with grace. Apparently it's a theme that remains mostly unsung.

The B.C. people and the A.D. people, they all dwell on the "giving" angle. Give! Give! Give! And it is still the cry.

"Better to give than to take," said John Heywood, somewhere between 1497 and 1580.

And, long before that, came the Biblical admonition: "It is more blessed to give than receive."

Call it good, proper, and explainable. Since the first dawn broke upon the first man, civilization has had a tendency to clench its fists and hold on to all it had. But we have improved. That prehistoric habit of devouring a whole bear—steaks, chops, and all—while the fellow in the next cave died of hunger . . . we are not that bad. Not any more.

There has been generation after generation brought up on the philosophy of sharing. And it has caught on. We give to the Red Cross. And we give to Goodwill. We give to the Salvation Army. And we give to the Community Fund. We give to the Heart Fund. And we give to the Red Door. We give to our churches. And we give to our clubs.

Give! Give! Give! By now it just comes naturally. The idea has been pounded into us for so long that we just give—and then stop to think later whether there is anything left with which to buy groceries. We have become a regiment of givers.

But we don't know the least about courtesy in receiving. We're baffled, confused, and half-way mad if a well-meaning acquaintance brings us a bag of beans from his garden. We are sure there's a catch to it—that the fellow either thinks we are broke, or he is getting all set to ask to borrow our lawnmower. And it isn't that at all. It's simply that, for a moment, the man has an urge to give. He's been trained to give, and give he must.

And anyhow, there is such a warm and luscious feeling attached to splitting the haul with the folks next door. The man has a yearning for that, too. But nothing doing. We refuse to grant to anyone else that delicious sensation of self-satisfaction. We are going to be the only people around here who give. So we go get our purse and offer to pull out some stinking little pieces of silver to pay for a mountain of generosity crowded into one small brown sack of Kentucky Wonders. Either that, or our brains begin a fast check of what possible gratuity we could return for said gratuity. A glass of jelly. No, a couple of glasses of jelly. A piece of a freshly made cake. No, that's too meager. The whole cake.

What a frightful need there is for simple, relaxed receiving. There have been tomes of instruction on the compensations resulting from an open hand. But few if any puny words on the matter of being a graceful recipient.

Everyone can't be on the giving end all the time—as delightful as that might be. Someone has to take. Someone has to be sweet and appreciative and willing. Yes, willing.

Let the do-gooders do good. And quit trying to get even. A sincere thank you is sufficient. The pleasure of giving is reward enough. And one turn doesn't necessarily demand another.

Resignation need not be unpleasant.

It can be a gentle adjustment to circumstances. After all, there are only two routes open: One can rave and stomp and curse the cross that one must bear. Or, one can face the thing with a kind of objectivity—like watching a sunset. It is possible to send up a white flag and learn to live at peace with a problem. Often that is all that is left by which to surmount the insurmountable.

13.

Scatter Ye Seeds

"Dinner is ready!" Hilda called from the kitchen. "And now don't poke around about coming. Hot biscuits are only fit to eat if they are hot!"

"Hot biscuits? Did you say hot biscuits?"

"I did. It's Mrs. Trimble's treat. She brought me a can of biscuits, and suggested that I fix them for all of us. They ought to go right good with chipped beef gravy." Hilda had come to the office, just off the kitchen, and was standing in the doorway with a big spoon in her hand.

Carrie Trimble, eighty-plus, always insisted on evening up the books when it came to gifts. Any little gratuity had to be paid off by another gratuity. The retired member of the staff of the Federal Reserve Bank in New York who had rented our front bedroom couldn't take without giving. This time she was settling up for a little serving of molded pineapple salad that had been put on her shelf in the refrigerator.

With her one daughter, Ruth, living in Indianapolis, this proud and regal lady, who stood so straight that she looked tall, had left the East to come to the Midwest. However, even at an advanced age, she insisted on maintaining her own quarters, separate and apart from her family.

It was one widow's solution as a way of life after an active business career. Hilda had also managed to adjust to a different manner of living. I was trying.

Perhaps it was in our mutual need that a warm fondness for one another had developed. We talked about it as we sat at the breakfast room table eating Mrs. Trimble's hot biscuits.

A nearby window looked out upon the far reaches of an October day. We agreed that between skylines and friendship there is a striking similarity.

In the far distance, earth and sky became one.

It was like a meeting of minds, where congenial views mingle in pleasant accord. Perhaps there were answers out there. Maybe one could put a query to that wide horizon, where purple haze hovered over golden and scarlet trees, a query something like this:

"Out of what is friendship made?"

Odd how we talk to that which has no tongue. But so we do. We look out into the night and ask about tomorrow. For ten thousand years and more, people have sought answers from the stars and whispered their yearnings to the breakers rolling in from the sea.

Perhaps it is because we are reticent. And we hesitate to lay open the cloak that hides our tremulous and uncertain self before those who might react lightly.

To ask just anyone, "What's a friend?" could bring forth a variety of replies. Maybe, such a one as this:

"A friend? Well, that depends. If you're a gal, a friend's a guy. And then, of course, the other way around."

Or still another might say: "I'm broke. Payday is a week away. Somebody slips me a few bucks. That's a friend."

Or again: "Why, don't you know? Your dog, that's your friend."

And so you tuck the query away, along with such perplexities as why do some leaves turn yellow and some leaves turn red. Or, how big is a man's soul?

And one day when you are out in a wild, untended field gathering milkweed pods for a winter bouquet, you feel the bigness of the universe that surrounds you. You also feel the insignificance of your own size.

It's still another time, wherein you toss your question into boundless space. And out of the silence flows the pattern of a friend.

Friendship is a fragile something marked, "Handle with Care"—yet as sturdy as dependability and as rugged as loyalty.

It's softly tender like love, and forgiveness, and hope—yet as hard as truth and as firm as faith.

Friendship is believing, when all others doubt. It's remembering, when all others have forgotten. It's rejoicing in another's good fortune, weeping for another's bad luck.

It's the man on the road to Jericho who goes where another is—and supplies what is needed, whether it's a word of encouragement or praise, or an invitation to come take a walk on a sunny autumn afternoon.

Somehow, a friend is intuitive and can sense a longing, and can come up with the right prescription to heal a headache, or comfort a hurt heart. A friend is someone whose spirit is nourished by the identical food that feeds our own; someone with whom we can find companionship even in silence, or with whom we can share differing convictions in a kind of tolerant understanding.

Because a friend looks upon you with affection and considers you someting special, you put forth a mighty effort to live up to the ideal. You try to do better, and are better—just because you have a friend.

The three of us whom events had brought together sat around the breakfast room talking for more than an hour after we had finished Carrie Trimble's hot biscuits and Hilda's chipped beef gravy. I had just started to pass out squares of the apple cake that I had made earlier in the day, when the door bell rang.

It was Bob Doeppers, chief photographer from the *News*, with a huge carton held between his two arms. He could hardly get through the door with his unwieldy burden.

"For goodness sakes, Bob, what have you got there?" I asked as he finally stepped inside.

The big blond young man with the quiet, genial manner was smiling: "The gals in the Women's Department," he said, "asked me to drop this off for you on my way home."

"Drop what?"

He set the box down and I pulled the two sections of the top apart and looked inside. The carton was filled with mail. There was one bundle of letters after another, tied up and squeezed into the overcrowded area of the cardboard container. The thing was bulging!

"What's the meaning of this?" I asked.

Bob shook his head. "I wouldn't know. The gals just said for me to drop it off," he repeated.

Out of the conglomeration of correspondence I lifted a letter. Scrawled on the face of the envelope, in pencil, were these lines:

> My Window
> Indianapolis News,
> Indianapolis, Ind.

Inside was a sheet of school tablet paper on which was written: "Dear friend: Saw your story about the Golden Rain Trees.

Please send me a few seed. Am sticking in a stamp for you to use, in sending them to me. Thank you lots. (Signed) Mrs. Maggie Hawkins." Then came the address.

Quickly I ripped open another one, and another one. All the while, Bob stood by looking puzzled and saying not a word. In sundry and varying manners, each letter made the identical request. Everyone was asking for a few Golden Rain seeds. The return addresses on any number of the envelopes were of well-known people. There was a professor from Purdue University. There was a man from the park department of another city. He wanted enough seed to plant a sizable grove in a community recreational area. There was a Campfire Girls' counselor. She wanted seed to pass out to all her young charges.

And there were more, indeed hundreds, of letters from ordinary people who simply wanted to plant a few seed with the hope of getting a Golden Rain Tree or two for their front yard.

Later, Mrs. Trimble and Hilda got up from the table and came out to look at the big box of letters.

"Do you have seed enough for all those people?" Mrs. Trimble asked.

"Twelve seed," I answered. "Just twelve seed."

"Twelve seed!" The two women fairly screamed out. "Twelve seed!"

It was real disconcerting.

No more than a week before, Anna P., a long-time friend of the column, had gotten a neighbor to drive her out to My Window for a little visit. Said Anna:

"I brought you a dozen Golden Rain seed, thought you might like to plant them. They are such beautiful trees. Bloom in June, you know . . . lovely little golden, orchid-like blossoms. The flowers keep falling to the ground. That's the meaning of the name, Golden Rain."

153

Anna continued to describe this interesting tree, and all the time she talked thoughts were racing. Perhaps a couple of readers of the column might like a seed or two to try. I did not need a whole dozen. Shortly thereafter, the following story appeared in My Window:

SEEDS FOR FREE—GOLDEN RAIN TREE SEED.

I have a few seed. And if, just for fun—you would like to try your hand at planting a golden rain tree, by way of seed, send along a self-addressed stamped envelope . . . .

All of us can thank Miss Anna P. for this somewhat novel opportunity of acquiring one of Hoosierdom's most famous trees.

It was, perhaps, 40 years ago that Anna's family planted its original rain tree from seed that had come from the campus of Indiana University.

The young rain trees that grow about Anna's home today are offspring of that first tree. The seed rained down and the "children" sprang up.

In fact, planting the seed is the surest and simplest way of getting a golden rain tree. Moving the trees is hazardous, owing to the tap root that early strikes down deep into the earth.

It is no small task to move such a tree and not disturb the all-important tap root.

But by merely scratching the soil lightly, and sowing a seed, covering it and marking the spot, you may one day be the possessor of a tree that will make you proud.

Indeed, the renowned golden rain trees of New Harmony, Indiana, were first planted as seed in that locality.

In 1828, William Maclure, while in Mexico, saw and immediately was caught up in ecstasy with the lovely trees. From that moment he became a kind of self-appointed distributor.

He sent seed to Thomas Say, of New Harmony—with the suggestion that they be planted by the gate of the Say home.

It was an ideal spot, because, like domesticated pets, the rain tree does best when near people. It prefers populated areas rather than the country and the woods. Today's countless rain trees in New Harmony had their beginning from those first seeds, planted by the Say gate.

In his "New Harmony Story" Don Blair writes: ". . . the rain tree reaffirms its beauty many times during the year. First, there is the beauty of line to be found in the shape of the bare limbs; next, there is the leafing out—when she shows her leaves, each a thing of joy; next there are the blooms, those golden blooms from which it gets its name, and which in turn are the golden drops in the golden shower."

Author Blair continued:

"Then come the variegated pods about the size of a lime and shaped like a Japanese Lantern. Again, after the pods are all shed, it takes its place with the other trees and is enhanced by its symmetry.

"At the end of the summer it, too, joins the parade costumed in autumnal colors."

It was easy to become enthused over the whole idea, since planting trees from seed had been a long-time interest at our house. Through the years, we had planted hickory nuts, buckeyes, chestnuts, walnuts, acorns, and pawpaws—and with encouraging results. The trees in many cases stand as proof.

Even as the column was folded up and placed in an envelope to be sent to the *News,* there came the earnest wish that at least someone might be interested in planting a Golden Rain Tree from seed. It would be nice to have company in the venture.

Now, with the enormous box of letters from the *News* office, the yearning was in another direction. The whole problem was how to get seeds for the company. Nothing was said, but three good people heard me thinking.

In fact, the morning after my invitation to share those few seed, a woman called from the west side of town. She said:

"We read your column in last night's paper. If you should need any more Golden Rain Tree seeds, we have a tree that is just laden with pods. If there is any way you could get out here and pick them up from the ground, you're welcome to them."

Later, a man from another area of town simply came to the

door, unannounced, toting a bushel basket of the little brown pods, seeds inside. And then, in the mail, came a small box of seeds already removed from their casing. With them a letter reading:

"Your offer to pass out a few Golden Rain Tree seeds was so appealing my wife and I feel that you are going to be swamped with requests. That's why we are sending you some seeds from our Golden Rain Tree. If you need more just say the word, and we'll send more."

The word was not long in coming.

Within a week, 1,535 letters asking for Golden Rain Tree seeds had come, and they continued to arrive. Hilda and Mrs. Trimble were wonderful about it all. They offered to help. And their offer was accepted.

The *News* wanted to get a picture of the great heap of mail. So another photographer from the paper came out with his equipment. Already the two ladies were chin deep in the letters, tearing them open, reading them, and removing self-addressed, stamped envelopes. The cameraman caught them in the act.

On the following day, there we all were on the front page of the Indianapolis *News,* with a sub-headline reading: "Raintree Seed Requests Pour In." As a result of this, another wave of mail arrived. There was no place to eat—the breakfast room table was inundated.

It was to be supposed that Hilda and Carrie Trimble would get something of a thrill out of landing on the front page. They took turns in looking at the picture of themselves. Both had been dressed in pastel housedresses, and, with their white hair, there was no contrast in color.

"We look like we are dead," Hilda said.

Said Mrs. Trimble: "Don't you dare let anybody see that picture of me."

"Why, Mrs. Trimble, I had planned on ordering some extra

copies, so you could send them to your sisters back East." I was disappointed. It had seemed such a nice reward for both Hilda's and Mrs. Trimble's willingness to come to the rescue.

But their endless belt procedure went on. The ladies developed a real system. All letters of an unusual nature, those that either asked for additional information or contributed some interesting commentary, were laid aside for a time when we could all participate.

Some of those writing had sent seeds from their own gardens. One reader put in a dime, another a dollar bill.

Special supplies had to be organized, like little enclosure envelopes in which to package the seed, and a sponge to be used in moistening envelopes. The latter was a late necessity, after everybody was getting sick at the stomach from licking the backs of envelopes before sealing. Still another need arose, in the matter of labels intended for the postman, labels reading: "HAND CANCEL." The whole cause would be lost if the fat, hard seeds jabbed a hole in the envelope enroute.

Because so many people had asked for specific planting instructions, it seemed the easiest way to reply would be by another column. This was reason for thought-taking, because every time the words "Golden Rain Tree seed" appeared in the paper, the mail would come rushing in immediately. At the moment, there was an overwhelming desire to avoid the name. Even seed philanthropy with others contributing the seeds could become rather expensive. After all, it was only right that Hilda and Mrs. Trimble have something for their time. Particularly when their pictures on the front page failed to offer any compensation pride-wise.

So it was, a whole column was devoted to the correct way to plant Golden Rain Tree seeds. Since the hard-shelled seeds needed the shock of freezing to break open their outer skin, it was suggested that they be planted outdoors in the earth during the autumn. That way the cold of winter would do the job. An alternative to this procedure was offered. To speed things up, one might put the Golden Rain Tree seeds in the water of an ice cube tray. Let them remain frozen in the ice cubes for a few days, and then take them out and plant them inside in a pot of soil. That way, by spring they would have sprouted and would be little seedling trees that could be set out in the garden.

It appeared to be a very clever idea, and proved successful in most instances. One woman, however, reported a catastrophe. She put her seeds in an ice cube tray to be frozen, but neglected to tell her husband. Company came, and in the course of his host duties he made cold drinks, using the ice cubes wherein abided the frozen Golden Rain Tree seeds.

He never noticed. Neither did the guests. And when the hostess went to wash the tumblers, there was no evidence of the seeds. All of which adds up to one conclusion: They went down along with the crushed ice and the drink. Well, since everybody was alive a week later, it would indicate that the free seeds were also edible.

While I have been chatting away in the column on sundry and assorted topics, other opportunities to hand out this and that advice to readers have arisen. Each time they have simply developed with the vein of discussion. A lady in Terre Haute wrote to the column expressing a long-time desire to locate a butterscotch pie recipe made with water instead of milk. Her inquiry later appeared.

Because of the kindness of a half-dozen readers, a half-dozen "Milkless Butterscotch Pie" recipes arrived by mail. Happy that the lady's wish for such a pie had been fulfilled, I duly reported the experience in the column. It was stated that the recipes would be sent to the woman who had made the request. If others were interested in butterscotch pies made with water they could write in for the recipes.

They did. This time, a package delivery truck pulled up at our house one night and brought a jam-packed box of letters from the *News*.

Later requests stuffed in manila envelopes continued to arrive, day after day, all mail forwarded from the paper. It happens every time, whether it's Love Apple seed, the huge Crawford County Tomato seed, homemade ice cream recipes, Red Hibiscus seed, lists of rare coins and their values, lists of old books that are now collectors' items. All of these things have been offered to readers, as occasion has come along. And with the offers have come a deluge of letters.

It never ceases to be thrilling. However, one old newspaper reporter who has been pounding his beat better than a half-century is not at all impressed:

"You'll learn," he said, "after a while, that if you offer to give away anything free, even one run-over-at-the-heel wornout shoe, there will be a stampede trying to take advantage of the chance!"

Maybe. But remember, if you are busy helping to stick seed in an envelope, you're not likely to be in a stew over what you haven't got, and what you wish you had.

Comes the word. It's Cousin Frank Harold. Grandpa Bush, out to spend a few days with Aunt Myrtie and Uncle Frank, had just joined Mamma and Papa. It had happened immediately following lunch. Laughing with a friend who had dropped by, he had collapsed and died. A great oak of a man, in both spirit and physique, who had weathered ninety-six springs was gone.

14.

Beyond This Place

Discouragement has been likened to many things. But this morning, looking out on the thick milky veil which obscures the view of familiar things, like Ross's house and Emily and Howard's house, it seems that discouragement is like the fog. Because of the gray curtain of drifting mist that hangs on every side, nothing is clear. Or sharp. Or distinct.

All is blurred—the fence that borders the drive, the road out yonder, the cars that pass.

It is like being lost in a kind of sea.

Only by reasoning and remembrance are the surroundings known to be unchanged, as always.

The top of the red mulberry tree out by the side of the barn is not gone. Not really.

It's just that the fog has blurred the outlook. The high limbs that crown the tree are still there. I know they are. It is just that I cannot see them. And the mailbox, some distance beyond the gate, has not disappeared. Not really. It is still there.

And the cardinal that calls from some place (I don't know from where) is not just a voice. He has a body—a trim and feathered scarlet figure. I am positive, and the thickest, most blinding fog cannot deceive me into thinking otherwise.

It's a truism. And it is something to which to cling when the way seems clouded and I grope in a haze of depression, doubt, and despair.

I remind myself: The landmarks from which I have for so long gathered strength have not forsaken me.

It's the fog.

Now and then, it happens to us all. Momentarily we lose our way in the mist of grief. Or we are befuddled into thinking that such things as kindness and tenderness and understanding can be misconstrued, can be questioned, can be lost from sight.

But faith is a lantern that lights the way.

And the unshaken confidence in ultimate happiness, affection and nobility becomes the seeing eyes that pierce the fog.

And they cannot be deluded by anything. They behold eternal, things as they forever are—eternal!

The late Fulton Oursler once wrote a little classic on the vital matter of attitude.

After all, what happens to us is of little note. It is how we take it.

To illustrate his point, the eloquent Oursler told this story:

In World War II a young soldier was badly injured. Lying on the operating table, the lad looked up at the surgeon, who said:

"It's all right, kid. You're going to get well. But I'm afraid   .   .   .   " The physician paused and started again. "I'm afraid you've lost your arm."

The boy smiled. And in a voice slightly more than a whisper he said: "I didn't lose my arm—I gave it."

No fog could dim his attitude.

Too often we sleep in a lethargy of passive acceptance. We need a rousing, vibrant realization of present potentials.

Your eyes—have you told yourself today that you are thankful for your eyes? They are important, your eyes. They tell you that the sun is shining, that a flock of chickadees is eating crumbs outside your window, that the neighbor across the way is hanging out her washing.

They are avenues of beauty, your eyes. They are portals through which pass sunsets and starlit skies and tall trees swaying in the wind. Because of your eyes you know the appeal of biscuits, golden brown, of red apples, and flames lapping up over a log fire. You know the look of a rose, the pink of a baby's cheek, the smile of the one you love.

By your eyes you gather entertainment and information, and walk with sages of ages past. You can look up at the new moon and watch it grow old. And you can look into a heap of debris and see the colors of the rainbow in a piece of broken glass.

Sometimes when everything seems awry and our world has all but fallen into bits, it helps to take stock. It helps to pause and evaluate the really priceless things—things like another's belief in us, things like our eyes.

In the constant race to snag a better job, more money, a bigger house, a second car—we overlook our current status. We forget to take into account the ability to sleep well, laugh heartily, and eat whatever is placed upon the table. A good digestion is more of an asset than a diamond tiara. And the sight of a yellow school bus unloading a flock of chattering boys and girls is one of the rewards of eyes.

Every so often we are confronted with those who have been deprived of things that other people take for granted. Who was it who said: "I cried because I had no shoes until I met a man who had no feet"?

Some time ago, Sue Andersen and I were with a group of

blind women. They were holding their monthly meeting, and from all over the city had come these people without sight.

An attractive woman was led in and guided to the seat beside me. She was dressed in lavender, with a hat that matched her frock. Her soft white hair framed a face that was gentle and serene.

We talked.

"How lovely you look," I said. "Your face is smooth and fair, without a wrinkle."

"Thank you," said the woman quietly. "I appreciate that a great deal, because I have not seen my face for thirty years."

In just a little while I was scheduled to speak to this group. And I asked myself: "What can one say to another who has not seen her face for thirty years? What can one say to those who have never seen; whose only picture of dawn is in their imagination; who gather the impressions of a petunia from their finger tips; and who have only a drop of water in their palm as evidence of a snowflake?"

Some time later, I talked with another woman, a woman who could see but whose son was blinded in World War II. His philosophy is characteristic of those who have become accustomed to the weight of their cross and even discover that it has its virtues.

Said the son: "Mother, you are fortunate. You can never grow old to me. You will never be one day older than the last day I saw you. That's the way I remember you and think of you."

He had found compensation in the lack of eyes. Do those who see, see as much?

However, there come times when we lose our way in the blackness of despair. It may be sorrow. It may be disappointment. It may be a seething, fermenting bitterness over the awful thing that has befallen us.

164

When courage hits bottom, what are we to do? What are we to do when all our world looks dreary and sober and sad?

It happens.

It happens to us all . . . sometimes, do what we may. There are days . . . we repeat, there are days when we fight for a light in the darkness as someone strangling struggles for air.

In an effort to explain our woes, we look out and around, over here and over there, trying to pinpoint the culprit. "If things were different," we say, "well, then we would feel better." Or, "So-and-so said such-and-such, and it is not so. . . . " Or, "The roof is leaking, and the furnace has gone bad; the car has a flat tire, and the rabbits are eating the crocuses."

We can find a million different places on which to place the blame. But of course this is no help. We need to grab hold of the chin of our doldrums and do a switch around. All of which leads us right, straight, head-on into a famous legend:

There was a king. He was crippled, and crooked, and deformed—in fact, he was a hunchback.

And because he was so ugly, he was rebellious—mean. He hobbled through his palace, bent over and scowling, trying to think of more cruel and oppressive laws he could lay upon his subjects.

One day, all unexpected, a sculptor appeared: "I pray thee, esteemed and exalted King," said the sculptor, "may I carve an image of your head—may I?"

Said the King: "Do me from the crown of my head to the soles of my feet—all of me, only without the curse. Make me as I might have been!"

And the sculptor agreed. Proud of his important commission, he made a statue of the King in white marble, a tall, straight, handsome figure—of goodly countenance and flawless form.

When it was delivered, the King ordered his statue to be put at the end of the garden by the pool. And every morning the King dragged himself down into the garden to look at his perfect self. For hours he would sit, beholding in rapt admiration the man "he wished he was."

This went on for years.

In time, the people of the kingdom began to ask one another: "What has happened to our ruler? He is different. He is kind now. He is gentle. He tries to help us."

And then one day somebody said: "His back . . . the King's back . . . it is not crooked anymore!"

The news spread. The King heard.

On the way down into the garden to look at the statue, he paused at the pool. In the water he could see his reflection, and he was erect and straight—no longer deformed. He looked like the perfect marble image. He had taken on the appearance of his "ideal self."

Ralph Waldo Emerson offered this prescription to anyone utterly weary and momentarily depressed:

"To the body and mind cramped by noxious work or company, nature is medicinal and restores their tone. The tradesman, the attorney comes out of the din and the craft of the street and sees the sky and the woods, and is a man again.

"In their eternal calm, he finds himself. The health of the eye demands a horizon. We are never tired so long as we see far enough."

Or, can sing.

There is amazing therapy in whistling, in humming, or, better, in breaking forth in a vocal outburst. No one can stay down long if he doggedly sings. When a heavy weight of depression settles down upon one, there is no quicker way to push off the load than to sing.

If you can't sing out loud, you can sing to yourself.

As one thinks of the melody and recalls the words, the train of thought is forced onto another track. It could even awaken an interest in the circumstances and events which inspired certain people to write some of our old and beloved songs.

For instance, there is the song "Lead Kindly Light" by John Henry Newman, who in his seventy-ninth year was named a cardinal. Earlier, however, in the time of unrest when he was being mistrusted and persecuted, Newman found himself reaching out for guidance.

Once, while aboard ship endeavoring to regain his health, he picked up his pen. Out of his anguish came a new resolve. He wrote:

> " . . . I love to choose and see my path:
> But now
> Lead Thou me on!"

Still another well-known song sprang from quite a different experience. John Fawcett (1731-1817) was just twenty-six when he became pastor of a little church in Wainsgate, England. For years he served his charge. But, caught between a small salary and a growing family, he decided to leave his flock for a better position in London.

The day came. The Fawcett family was packed, ready to move. The village folk came to say goodbye. They were weeping. The Fawcetts were shocked. They had no idea their departure would bring such sadness. Said Mrs. Fawcett: "Let's stay." The pastor was quick to agree.

The pastor was grateful for the tenderness and love expressed. His warm and affectionate sentiments were set forth on paper— set forth in a poem called, "Blest Be the Tie That Binds."

It was the beauty of wheat fields and "fruited plains" that excited Katherine Lee Bates. An English teacher at Wellesley

College, she was on her way to Colorado where she was to teach one summer. The loveliness of the western country thrilled her. The purple majesty of the mountains and the spacious skies made a deep and lasting impression. In fact, the exaltation was still with her some four years later when she wrote, "America, the Beautiful."

Writer Sarah Flower Adams had not planned to be a writer. She was an actress. But failing health turned her efforts into this other channel. Seeking encouragement, some thread of hope to which she might cling, she penned a mighty portrayal of a great faith. In the course of the years, untold numbers of human beings have gathered comfort from the particular song which Mrs. Adams wrote. President William McKinley was heard singing it very softly as he lay dying. Then there was that other gripping event that had to do with this particular hymn. The *Titantic* was on its maiden voyage. It struck an iceberg. As it was sinking, the ship's band played until the freezing waters closed over them. They played Sarah Flower Adams' song—"Nearer, My God, to Thee."

All of this serves to remind us that prayers are not just those words muttered as we bow our heads and kneel on bended knee.

That kind is important, of course, but so are those that are active and working—the sort that show forth the goodness of one's Maker in a job well done.

"Order," said the poet, "is heaven's first law." That being the case, an orderly house must be a link between earthly creatures and their eternal dwelling place. To that degree, at least, they have a connection that runs from earth to heaven. Glasses rubbed to a dazzling shine, then placed in even rows on a cupboard shelf. Table tops that are without spot; a floor freshly scrubbed. That's a prayer.

Work is also therapy.

Really, there are no menial chores. Every task is an opportunity to bring a little bit of perfection into an imperfect world. A well-made bed. Clothes washed clean. A patch set neatly on a worn garment. There is a right way to do everything—everything from washing a baby's face to erecting a skyscraper. And when a job is done right, one has the O.K. of his conscience. And that is living in accord with best standards. That's prayer—prayer in action.

They talk about charity, about loving one's neighbor as one's self. A good idea . . . one that we tie up with Sunday School and church, a preacher and his sermon. And yet, that, too, is a moving, lively force that penetrates the common routine of every day. It shows up in punctuality . . . in being on time for appointments. It makes itself evident in carefully and meticulously preparing a meal, and serving it with beauty and a certain flair. It pays bills promptly. And remembers to speak its thanks for a favor.

Prayers are not just pretty pieces reserved for the Sabbath. They are the silent companions of the carpenter, the bricklayer, the office stenographer. There is a moment, one brief, swift interval, when the worker confers with his thoughts: Shall he run the plane a little longer and make the board even more smooth? Shall he put the level on the block wall yet once again and check for perfect level? Shall the typist let the smudged sheet go on its way, or shall she make a fresh, clean copy?

These are moments of beseeching, when frail humanity puts itself on trial. The job will be done well or it will be done poorly. The choice lies with the doer. And glory to the one who is his own master.

In proper behavior we see a prayer. Those people whom we label as successes have become so because they did many things right. They said many prayers.

I remembered Lelia. She was our cleaning lady. Said Lelia: "I was just going to leave that one wee spider and his little web in the corner of the spare room. My broom and cleaning things had been put away. And then I thought—why, by next time I come to clean, that spider might have spun his web clear across one end of the room, might even have the door roped off so I couldn't get in. That finished it. I went and got my broom and cloth and wiped down the spider and the web."

Lelia had lived a prayer.

Probably the first step out of the place in which we now find ourselves is at the threshold of our own outlook. Always, when things go awry, when unhappiness comes, frustration and grief—we believe that help lies out there. We forget that often the control panel for "out there" is within our own minds and hearts.

Nine times out of ten, a change within brings about a change without.

I love the story (a true one) of a saloon keeper who most earnestly and sincerely embraced the Christian faith. Completely in accord with every religious principle of his chosen church, he was distressed with his lot as a saloon keeper. Immediately, he offered the business for sale—putting up a big sign in the window, and placing a large advertisement in the town paper.

He was ready for the first buyer who came along. There was nothing he wanted more than to get out from behind that bar, and to stop contributing to the debauchery of people.

But no buyer came.

Try as he might, no one appeared. After months and months of effort, there was no change—no prospect of a purchaser. The saloon keeper was in the same groove and with no hope of release.

He talked with some of his more devout church friends, asking for their advice and their prayers. He couldn't just walk away from his investment and abandon it. All the money he had was tied up in his business.

Finally, after much discussion and deliberation—yea, and asking guidance from above—this procedure was agreed upon: The saloon keeper would go on with his business, only with this alteration in affairs—he would make every effort to be a better saloon keeper. He would try to improve his location and better his service.

And so he did.

Straight off, he painted the front. He washed the windows. He scrubbed the floors, and he put in a new bar and stools. And besides all this, he stopped hating the place and the derelicts who came in and the turn of fate which had trapped him in such a situation.

He even sang when nobody was around, when, momentarily, the saloon was empty. And dozens of times each day, he found things for which he could be thankful—things like two good legs on which he could stand as he worked; two good arms with which he could lift down a bottle of liquor and fill up a glass; two good eyes by which he could see into the faces of those who came for a drink.

Often he could detect a desperate yearning to do better, but a bewilderment as to where to turn. Again and again, the man behind the bar spoke some Biblical word of strength and encouragement as he waited on a customer, words like:

"Great is our Lord, and of great power: his understanding is infinite." (Psalms 147:5)

Inconsistent? Not at all. The point for help is at the place of need.

Three months from the time the man bent all efforts to be a better saloon keeper, the representative of a big brewery stopped in with a proposition. His company wanted to open a regional office. They were willing to pay a price to get that particular spot.

By endeavoring to do the very best he could at the place in which he found himself—the saloon keeper made his escape.

15.

Hither, Thither, The Promise

The scene shifts . . . yes, it shifts, but there is another scene. Not the same one, to be sure; not the first warm and endearing one in which you opened your eyes, and in which you later grew up. But even so, another scene, inhabited by kindly folk who, in their way, minister to your need . . . comfort, love, and run in to see if there is a My Window column to mail to the *News*.

Again and again, Lorraine does just that. She is our neighbor a couple of miles to the north. And sometimes, on her way to the cleaners or to take one of the children to the dentist or to deliver her own daily script to a local television station, she will stop.

Florence Eby is just east a piece. Every week she phones: "Going to the grocery," she says. "Got an order ready for me?" She comes back loaded with big brown bags out of which stick bread, and bacon, and maybe a cellophane bag of cranberries. And not infrequently, tucked in as a surprise, a loaf of her Pennsylvania pudding meat, or Philadelphia scrapple.

Let it snow, and Mr. Whitfield, who is retired, walks over with his shovel and opens up a path from our front door to the side gate, and then out to the street.

Throughout the summer, the Glancys appear at the door with armloads of vegetables. It starts with the first green onions and crisp, ruffled leaves of lettuce. And it continues through the days of snap beans and tomatoes, sweet corn and squash. With school out, Leonard Glancy, who is a teacher, spends his free time gardening a great plot of rich brown earth that extends 'longside the Glancys' house.

And then there is Carol. She teaches, too. And, like Lorraine, is married with young children. And yet she finds time to bake all sorts of yummy things . . . pies on which the meringue is piled inches high, plus cookies, plus bread. On a Saturday, she will run in with not just one sample of her baking, but a great array of oven delicacies . . . even homemade cream puffs.

This spontaneous outpouring of goodness from the hands and hearts of all these different people recalls an experience of several years ago. My friend Kay S. was elected to the presidency of our local chapter of the National League of American Penwomen. Immediately afterwards, and just at the close of the meeting, I chanced upon Kay and the outgoing president, the late and much-loved Miss Ella Sengenberger, talking together. Said Kay:

"I can never fill your shoes."

Even as I moved on, the remaining conversation followed me.

"No, you cannot," replied the ever humble and always selfless Miss Sengenberger.

It was so wholly unlike that lady whom we all held in such esteem and respect that I could not help but feel shocked. And then Ella Sengenberger continued:

"No one ever fills the shoes of another," she said. "You will fill the post in your own very wonderful and efficient way."

Apparently this has happened. Different people here and

there have, in all gentleness, slipped onto the present stage of experience. Their roles are in no way like the parts performed by those now gone. That is impossible, too much to expect. But in a multitude of ways, others take a place in the present pattern, providing an opportunity to encourage and be encouraged, to lift and be lifted.

Breakfast was scarcely over, one bright autumn morning, when the telephone rang. Said a lady, sprightly, eagerly: "I'm Ruth Lyons, of the 50-50 Club in Cincinnati." Continued the voice in my ear: "A reader of your column has sent me your little book, *Parade of Days*. And I would like to talk about it on my television show today."

Trying to latch onto a reason for this sudden and unexpected turn of events, I replied: "You say a reader of My Window column sent it to you? Did they give their name?"

Said Miss Lyons: "Here's the letter that came with the book. The name is Rainey . . . George Rainey. He says, 'My wife and I listen to your program every day, and we think you would enjoy this book.' " There was a pause:

"And I did. I took it home with me from the studio yesterday, and read it before I went to bed last night. I used almost a whole box of Kleenex. But still I loved it."

The caller continued: "Usually, when I speak of something, you know, some particular item, the television audience likes to know where they can buy it. What do I tell them?"

"Why . . ." I was stunned dumb.

Miss Lyons was talking again: "Couldn't I just tell people to write to the *News* . . . the Indianapolis *News*?"

That afternoon it happened. During the widely viewed 50-50 Club, which emanated from WLW-TV in Cincinnati, Miss Lyons talked about the book. She even played a musical background on the organ while her mellow-voiced announcer, Peter Grant, read a selection from the small volume.

Within a couple of hours, local book stores were phoning. Customers had come in looking for *Parade of Days*. Before a week had passed, there were bushel baskets of mail at the office of the Indianapolis *News*. And practically every letter had either currency or a check enclosed. With Christmas not too far away, people were wanting the book for Yuletide giving.

Now all there was to do was to get in touch with the printing firm and beg them to hurry up and print some books. It had been privately published some years earlier, and there were just a few dozen copies stuck back in a closet.

The printing firm leaped into the effort, even to working nights, endeavoring to turn out a second printing—and fast! They made it—and almost a week before Christmas. However, within less than six months it was necessary to get out a third printing. People kept writing. Orders kept coming. The fabulous Ruth Lyons, beloved by a TV audience of housewives throughout the Midwest, had wrought a miracle—an electrifying one!

Two years later, with the publication of another book, *I Am Only One*,* Ruth spoke out again. And once more her viewers responded.

This star saleslady of the air, now retired, had all unexpectedly reached around and planted meaning in a life. So had the reader who had wrapped a simple little book up in brown paper and sent it off to her.

Just now, as I sat in a Ford station wagon holding eleven-week-old Bruce Anthony in my arms, events of the past few years came to mind.

Moments before, the whole family had left the car to watch undefeated Northview Junior High School's football team play undefeated Carmel Junior High. Our Alan, who had been just

---

The Bobbs-Merrill Co., Inc., 1963

an infant when Papa passed away, was now fourteen years old. He was playing left guard on Northview's first string.

Almost as tall as his father, and weighing a solid 180 pounds, he, like his brother Bruce, now nineteen, liked being an uncle to their sister Cynthia's little son, Bruce Anthony.

Once again, thoughts took off in still another epical phase. It was an easy thing to do, with just the baby and me in the car. Everyone had thought that the November afternoon was entirely too chilly for Bruce Anthony to take his place on the bleachers. So, not understanding football too well, I was glad for the chance to stay with the baby.

The little one, cuddled into his blue satin baby bunting suit, peacefully pulled on his bottle. We were both confident that his Uncle Alan's team would come through.

The news had come as a real jolt.

Our Cynthia, brother Syd and Louise's daughter, was at New Mexico State University, on the second lap of her Peace Corps training.

We should have known it could happen. When a woman of twenty-three, with dancing eyes and auburn hair piled high on her head, goes forth into the wide, wide world, she is not likely to go unnoticed.

But somehow, that had not come into our minds. So it was nothing short of shocking when the following letter arrived from Cynthia:

Dear Mother and Daddy,
  Because I know how very happy you two have been together through the years, I know you will be happy for me now
  . . . . Last night, Chandler, of whom you have heard me speak so often, one of our Peace Corps trainees, asked me to be his wife, and I said, "Yes." Now I know this comes as a great surprise

177

to you both, but I hope and pray for your blessing. . . . He is a wonderful person, and I love him very much. . . . This morning, we talked with the officials of the Peace Corps, and they were pleased to hear the news. They said that, in many ways, they felt it was better for married couples to go into the host countries rather than single people, because a married couple is much more stable. . . .

Immediately thereafter, a letter came from Chandler to Cynthia's parents. It read:

. . . I have asked your daughter to be my wife because I love her. . . . Cyndy has all of the qualities which will make me very happy—the qualities of love, compassion, sympathy, and understanding, which I have never before found in any one girl. . . . I want you both to know that our pending marriage will not affect- our plans to continue in the Peace Corps program, and spend the next two years in El Salvador. . . .

Chandler, the son of Mr. and Mrs. Paul Johnson of North Providence, R.I., was as dedicated to the Peace Corps as the girl he had asked to be his wife.

A graduate of the University of Rhode Island, with a degree in horticulture, he was to teach gardening to El Salvador's young people. Cynthia would teach sewing, cooking, and home improvement. Their interests could not be more happily allied.

Syd and Louise flew down for the wedding. They had wanted to get there a few hours ahead of the ceremony to get acquainted with the young man who was about to join the family. But a fog slowed down transportation and they arrived at the 150-year-old Episcopal Church in Mesilla Park, New Mexico, just five minutes before the wedding march began.

The little church was filled with Peace Corps officials, professors and their wives from New Mexico State University, and Peace Corps trainees.

In the candlelight, one tremulous daddy, trying hard to swallow back the big lump that kept rising in his throat, walked his one daughter down the aisle.

Came the traditional query: "Who giveth this woman to be wed to this man?"

Said Syd softly, serenely, "Her mother and I."

There was no holding back life and its unfolding chapters—yea, though it was to lead our young people so far away as Zacatecoluca, El Salvador, in Central America.

But the two years passed. Time does that. It was the following summer, after they had returned, when Bruce Anthony arrived.

I looked down at him now sleeping soundly, his pink little mouth still holding onto the nipple and the now empty bottle.

Cheerleaders were yelling. Even from afar, you could see middle-aged men, gray-haired women, mothers and fathers, teachers and youngsters from both schools leaping to their feet from time to time.

The babe slept on. In fact, he was still sleeping when the family came galloping over to the car, all of them grinning broadly.

"Uncle Alan's" team had won. It was Northview 26, Carmel 6.

Later, there was ice cream, a long fancy cake marked off as a football field, and soft drinks. But not before Coach Stiles, of Northview, got the dunking of his life, the victory plunge, when his hilarious, happy team put him in the shower.

On the way home, the words of the Psalmist kept singing in my thoughts: "When my father and my mother forsake me, then the Lord will take me up."

Maybe this was the way it worked. When people lost their dear ones, whatever the relationship, He who watched over the universe would provide this interest and that, to help fill the awful emptiness. Even sitting on the sidelines looking on could be absorbing.

Was it possible that this could be a first step in finding contentment within one's self? Perhaps this was the ultimate of honest-to-goodness fulfillment. That yearning cry, calling out in the moment of loss: "Where is everybody?" could eventually find an answer, at the place whereon one stood.

It could be that the only solution was in living happily with whatever happiness one could find.

Sometimes, joy is no more than a light that comes on inside of you, when you are thankful for your eyes that see, your bed to lie down in when you are tired, a roof to cover you when it is raining.

Joy is in being hungry and having something to eat.

Joy is in loving everybody, and not hating yourself.

Joy is in waking up in the morning and hearing country noises—things like a hen cackling over the achievement of an egg; a cow mooing for her calf and the calf mooing back; and the sound of a state highway mower slashing the tall weeds down along the road.

Joy is having more to do than you can possibly get done, and liking what you have to do.

Joy is the hallelujah feeling of polishing off a job that you had put off entirely too long.

Joy is in sitting down and writing a letter. Joy is in getting a letter at last.

Joy is in lifting the telephone receiver and hearing a dear and familiar voice.

Joy is the neighbor across the way, running in with a pan of just-made apple dumplings. Joy is in our running across to the neighbor, with anything from a jar of pickles to a bouquet of purple asters.

Joy is the first tomato from the garden—plump and red, and weighing two and a half pounds. Joy is in giving away the seed from these super-size specimens to anyone who would like some.

Joy is in having company for supper, and then later sitting on the front porch and watching the moon slip in and out from behind clouds.

Joy is in a whippoorwill calling from away off.

Joy is one lone katydid saying his name over again and again.

Joy is in the peace of a household at rest . . . the rhythmic ticking of the clock in the front hall.

Joy is in dreaming of impossible joys.

Joy is in hoping—always a priceless luxury.

Joy is in having something to which to look forward, and in having memories on which to look back.

Joy is in trying to attain that which we have always desired . . . through work, through striving, through struggle.

Joy is in knowing when to give up and cease fighting and take with grace what fate has destined for us.

Joy is not only in accepting things as they are, but also in not feeling too badly over what they might have been.

Joy is in turning the key in your own door. Joy is the wild welcome of your dog when the door opens.

Joy is in not being afraid.

Joy is a feeling that you are encircled in warmth and tenderness, even when you are all alone.

Joy is odds and ends . . . bright pebbles lying here and there on our path that we stumble over unless we look for them.

Hilda met me at the door: "I have just had a call," she said, "from the Indianapolis Home for the Aged. My name has come up. And they have accepted my application, and are ready for me to enter."

"Oh, no!" I dropped down into a chair. The matter had been in the offing for a long time, something that Hilda had intended to do when she got old. But that would never happen. Hilda was going to always be young.

"I'm seventy-five," she said. "And going into a retirement home is something a person has to do when she is well and able to get about. . . . "

Said Mrs. Trimble at breakfast: "Hilda is smart. I have been writing around, too, gathering information. Next week I'm going down to visit the Kennedy Memorial Home at Martinsville. The years pass, and we have to make provisions for them. . . ."

I was about to be alone again.

Sitting at my window, I watched the last rust-brown leaves from the cottonwood break away from twig and branch and drift to the ground. 'Twas the sequence of the seasons. But in their departure, they left a promise.

After the winter, the spring.

Single women